HISTORY OF THE WORLD

VOLUME VI

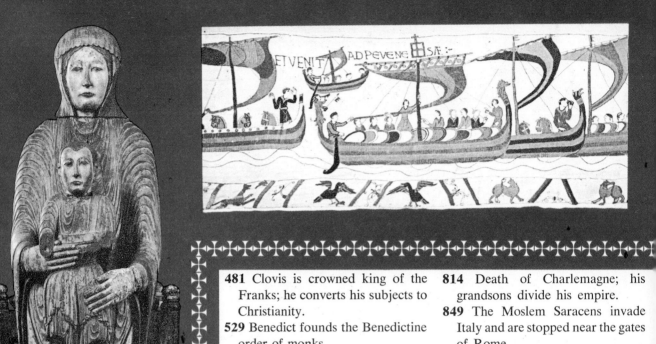

481 Clovis is crowned king of the Franks; he converts his subjects to Christianity.

529 Benedict founds the Benedictine order of monks.

752 Pepin the Short, first of the Carolingians, is elected king of the Franks.

771 Charlemagne, son of Pepin, succeeds him and adds to the kingdom through wars of conquest.

778 Charlemagne is defeated at Roncesvalles in Spain by Moslems.

800 Charlemagne is crowned Holy Roman Emperor by the pope.

814 Death of Charlemagne; his grandsons divide his empire.

849 The Moslem Saracens invade Italy and are stopped near the gates of Rome.

871 Alfred the Great of England defeats the Danish invaders.

885 Norsemen besiege Paris but the defenders, led by the Count of Paris, drive them away.

910 The monastery of Cluny is founded and begins a reform movement in the church.

911 Norsemen are given permission to settle part of France.

933 The German army stops the invasions of Magyars.

962 Otto the Great of Germany is crowned Holy Roman Emperor.

987 Hugh Capet, Count of Paris, is crowned king of France, founding a dynasty lasting 800 years.

1016 Canute, a Dane, seizes the English throne.

1066 William, duke of Normandy, invades England and defeats King Harold at the battle of Hastings.

1077 Henry IV of Germany is excommunicated and begs the pope's forgiveness at Canossa.

1096 Pope Urban II calls for a holy war to free Jerusalem; the first crusade begins.

1099 Crusaders capture Jerusalem from the Saracens.

1122 The Concordat of Worms settles the dispute between the emperor and the pope.

1147 The second crusade.

1152 Frederick Barbarossa becomes emperor; Henry of Anjou marries Eleanor of Acquitaine, uniting much of France under his rule.

1154 Henry of Anjou becomes the first Plantagenet king of England.

HISTORY OF

Editor Irwin Shapiro

Associate Editor Jonathan Bartlett

Consultant Albert Fried,
*Department of History,
Queens College, New York*

Contributors Anne Howard Bailey

John Bowman

Ormonde de Kay, Jr.

Edith Firoozi

Albert Fried

Johanna Johnston

Ira N. Klein

Willis Lindquist

Edna Ritchie

Seymour Reit

James L. Steffensen

VOLUME VI

THE UNIVERSAL
THE WORLD

THE WEST IN THE MIDDLE AGES

*by Anne Bailey and
Seymour Reit*

GOLDEN PRESS NEW YORK

CONTENTS

THE VISIGOTHS MASSACRED THE ROMAN LEGIONS AT ADRIANOPLE.

The End and the Beginning

378-752

THE FIRST SIGN of the approaching Roman army was a thin column of dust. It rose like smoke from behind the jagged Thracian hills of Northern Greece, which sheltered the Visigoths' encampment. Moments later, the Visigoths, or German barbarians, as the Romans called them, could feel the ground tremble with the tread of the imperial legions. The Romans were advancing, forty thousand strong, under the personal command of the Emperor Valens.

Within the Visigoths' barricade of wagons, all was confusion. Chieftains bellowed, calling their clans together. Sturdy Visigothic warriors dragged the wagons closer together in a protective circle. Horses neighed and whinnied as their riders leaped astride them; swords were unsheathed and lances brandished. A courier spurred away from camp to summon the main body of Visigothic cavalry, foraging at some

438

THIS CRUSHING DEFEAT MARKED THE BEGINNING OF ROME'S FALL.

distance. It was A.D. 378, and the battle of Adrianople was about to begin.

Trumpets blared, and the close-packed Romans marched straight toward the barbarian enemy. Suddenly, there was a thunder of hooves on the left. A great swarm of Visigothic horsemen, summoned from their foraging expedition, galloped over the hillside. They swooped down on the Romans, as an eyewitness described it, "like a thunderbolt which strikes on a mountain top, and dashes away all that stands in its path." More horsemen poured in from the right and the front, pressing the tightly massed Romans into a death trap. The men of the legions could scarcely raise their arms to strike a blow. Again and again the horsemen charged, brandishing lance and sword. When night fell, forty thousand Roman soldiers lay dead upon the field, together with the grand master of the infantry and cavalry, the count of the palace, thirty five commanders of horse and foot corps, and the Emperor Valens himself. This great defeat was to mark the beginning of the end of the mighty Roman Empire.

The city of Rome had been the cornerstone of the Roman empire for centuries. Rome controlled most of the then known world—Italy, Spain, Gaul (Modern France), Switzerland, Belgium, and large parts of Britain, Germany, Austria, the

THE LEGIONS TRAINED CONSTANTLY WHILE GUARDING THE EMPIRE'S FRONTIERS.

Balkans, Greece, Asia Minor, the near East, Egypt, and North Africa. Roman legions guarded the colonies. Roman justice prevailed in the courts. Roman customs were admired and copied. Even a succession of weak emperors had not disturbed the order and stability of Roman civilization, and Roman citizens believed they would always enjoy security. And then came their defeat by the Visigoths at Adrianople.

THE BARBARIANS

The Visigoths were only one of the many German tribes which had drifted down from the forests and marshes of northern Europe. There were also the Ostrogoths, Franks, Alemanni, Burgundians, Lombards, and Vandals. As early as 50 B.C., Julius Caesar had recognized that these tribes could be dangerous enemies. He

had laid down a rule that under no circumstances were they to be allowed to cross the Rhine or Danube rivers.

The German barbarians were fierce, restless people, and hardy warriors. Tall, blue-eyed, with tangled reddish-blond hair, they were described as giving over their time "to sleep and eating" when not at war or engaged in hunting. They were men of action, not thought. They lived in huts of rough-hewn timbers, or in caves, and clothed themselves in animal skins. Although they owned animals, and farmed here and there, they mostly lived a nomadic life, moving from place to place.

Within a tribe were several clans. Each was ruled by a chieftain, chosen for his ancestry and valor. These early German chiefs, or kings, did not have unlimited power. They were expected to lead by example, and their decisions could be overruled by a vote of the free warriors of the

441

clan. Each clan was held responsible for the offenses and crimes of its members, and this led to many interclan feuds and tribal wars. The unforgivable crime was cowardice. It was a disgrace for a warrior to leave his shield on the battlefield without dying beside it.

Because the Germans loved war and hunting, they also loved weapons. They had heavy battle axes of metal or stone, daggers, spears, bows, and short swords called *seax* (from which the word Saxon probably comes). They went into battle protected merely by light chest plates of brass-studded leather. Sometimes they wore no clothes at all. They often rushed to attack singing loudly in their hoarse, deep voices, terrifying their enemies.

The Germans' pagan gods were super-beings who also reveled in war and the hunt. Among them were Tyr, the war god, and Thor, the thunder god who wielded a mighty ax. Thor was worshipped on a special day of the week—Thorsday, or Thursday. Wodensday, or Wednesday, was sacred to Woden, or Wotan, the all-powerful and all-wise guardian of the land and law and order. Wotan was also Lord of Valhalla, the place to which dead heroes were carried by warrior maidens, the Valkyries, there to feast and fight throughout eternity.

MIGRATIONS OF THE TRIBES

More than 150 years before the battle of Adrianople, the various German tribes began to push down from their tree-choked, swampy northern lands toward the frontiers of the Roman empire. The Visigoths moved southward in Western Europe. In the east, near the Black Sea, the Ostrogoths migrated toward the Balkans. With them they brought a device called stirrups, which enabled a man to use a horse as an instrument of battle. The Goths quickly adopted the innovation, which was to change the entire character of warfare. Indeed, the Gothic horseman was to be the ancestor of the mounted knight of the Middle Ages.

As the Visigoths and the Ostrogoths, together with the Salian Franks in the area of the Rhine, the Vandals in Hungary, and other tribes across Europe, pressed south toward the Roman borders, seeking new grazing lands, a warmer climate, or escape from hostile neighbors, the Romans re-

laxed their age-old rule. They permitted the barbarians to cross over the frontiers. Soon, Roman commanders were gladly accepting German warriors as recruits in Roman armies. The Roman government permitted German colonists to settle on public lands or cultivate unused fields of private landowners inside the borders of the empire. By A.D. 378, the former barbarians made up a large part of the Roman military force and held important positions in the Roman government.

ATTILA THE HUN

It is possible that the German barbarians might have become absorbed into the Roman Empire without violence, if a new and savage group of nomads had not appeared on the scene. They were the Huns, who swept west from the Asian steppes, spreading death and destruction. Europe had known nothing like them before. Described as "fiercer than ferocity itself," the Huns poured across China, central Asia, and Russia, and pushed on into Europe. Wherever they went, the left behind them ravaged fields, smoking ruins, and countless dead. The Hun warriors spent their lives on horseback; there, an early historian wrote, "they buy and sell, they take their meat and drink, and there they recline on the narrow neck of their steed." Their scarred weather-beaten faces, their garments made of foul-smelling leather, their rat-skin helmets, terrified all who saw them. The Huns' most famous leader, Attila, was called the "scourge of God"—his horrified victims believed God had sent him as punishment for their sins. From his palace court in Hungary he ruled over millions of square miles, and held the power of life and death over half the known world.

To escape the terrible Huns, the Visigoths asked permission of the Roman Emperor Valens to settle in the empire. He said they could enter Northern Greece, provided they gave hostages and surrendered their arms. But the Roman officials in charge of the Gothic settlements accepted bribes and allowed the tribesmen to keep their arms. In addition, the Romans cheated the Visigoths by selling them food at extremely high prices. The Visigoths rebelled, and a Roman army was sent to push them back to the frontier. The army failed, and in A.D. 378 Valens person-

ROMAN FOOT SOLDIERS WERE FORCED TO GIVE WAY BEFORE THE HARD-RIDING HUNS.

ally took command of his legions. He marched to Adrianople, confident that he would defeat the Visigoths and their allies, the Ostrogoths. After all, Roman armies had always defeated the barbarians. This time, however, it was the Romans who were defeated, and for the next few generations, hordes of barbarians would pour across the empire's borders and even invade the city of Rome.

The Romans themselves did not realize that their civilization was about to fall apart. After the first shock of the defeat at Adrianople, they again took up the routine of their lives. Crowds swarmed to the Colosseum to watch the games; Roman gentlemen argued politics in the Forum and Roman ladies gossiped about the latest fashions.

But the Visigoths were on the move, united under a fearless chieftain named Alaric. He attacked Constantinople, but when he failed to conquer the city, he slowly moved his armies toward Italy. Meanwhile, the Vandals, after ravaging Gaul for three years, moved south into Spain, and the Franks, Burgundians, and Alemanni spread to Germany and Gaul. Little by little, Rome was being encircled by the barbarian tribes.

The Huns renewed their pressure in the East, and Alaric tried to escape them. He asked permission from the Roman emperor to move his Visigoth tribes south to Italy. He also demanded payment for the military help his people had given the Romans. When the emperor refused his demands, Alaric marched on Rome, and in A.D. 410, the Visigoths sacked the capital.

"TOMB OF THE PEOPLES"

Shock waves rippled to the remotest corners of the empire. By this time Christianity had been the official religion of Rome and her provinces

443

for more than a hundred years, and the Christian leaders were horrified. St. Jerome, who was translating the Hebrew Scriptures into Latin, grieved that the "mother (Rome) should become the tomb of the peoples." St. Augustine undertook his mightiest work, *The City of God,* to prove that Christianity was not responsible for the evil things that were happening.

THE EMPIRE FALLS

A year after his sack of Rome, Alaric died, and the city and the empire breathed easier. The Visigoths were given south central Gaul for their own lands, and from there they spread into Spain. The Vandals, meantime, had crossed the narrow Straits of Gibraltar from Spain to North Africa. At first allies of Rome, they finally turned against her, led by their small, lame, merciless king, Gaiseric. In 455, Gaiseric's Vandals invaded Rome; for two weeks they plundered, burned, looted and killed. From their senseless and vicious destruction of civic buildings and priceless works of art comes the word "vandalism," meaning the malicious destruction of useful or beautiful things.

The empire now sank into despair and confusion; political power belonged to whoever could grab fastest and hang on hardest. For the next thirty years, German chieftains killed and deposed one another in a constant struggle to rule Rome and Italy. Elsewhere, the frontier territories were being broken up into separate states. Lombards held the north of Italy. The Visigoths held Spain and Southern Gaul. Salian Franks ruled central and northern Gaul, and beyond them, to the east, were the Ripaurian Franks and the Alemanni. The Burgundians dominated the Rhône Valley, and the Vandals were spread out across the rim of North Africa.

In Britain, after the withdrawal of Roman troops, the land was overrun by tribes of savage Picts, Scots, and Saxons. After almost 400 years of Roman rule, the Britons had forgotten how to defend themselves. They tried to stem the invasion of their land, but they were no match for the fierce barbarians. The worst of the barbarians were the Saxons. A fearful Briton described them as "ferocious . . . of unspeakable name, hateful to God and man."

Centralized government broke down completely. Commerce and trade were at a standstill. Roads crumbled into ruin or were unsafe for travel because of cutthroats. Handsome and luxurious cities built by the Romans, such as Bath, were abandoned and became the haunt of bats and small night animals. Villages were attacked and burned; families massacred or scattered. Crops rotted in the fields or on the vines because there was no one to harvest them; the farmers were dead or in hiding. Schools were

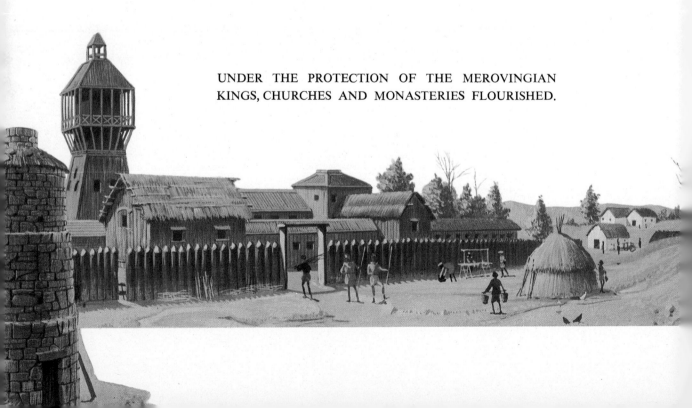

UNDER THE PROTECTION OF THE MEROVINGIAN KINGS, CHURCHES AND MONASTERIES FLOURISHED.

shut down. Churches stopped holding services. The Britons huddled in caves, or fled to the mountains of Wales, or escaped to Brittany. They complained to God: "Thou lettest us be eaten up like sheep, and hast scattered us amongst the heathen."

THE DARK AGES

Furthermore, what happened in Britain also happened elsewhere; there was desolation everywhere in Europe. Few remnants of Roman civilization survived. Towns and roads fell into ruin, and the people were often hungry. Brigands roamed the countryside, and it seemed that the disorder would never end. This time, which would last for 400 years, came to be called the Dark Ages. And yet, in 481, only twenty years after the sack of Rome by the Vandals, the Salian Franks crowned a king who was to lay the foundation for Western Europe as it is today.

This king, whose name was Clovis, was of the line of Merovingian kings descended from Meroveus, ruler of the Salian Franks. The Franks, unlike the Visigoths, Ostrogoths, and other Germanic tribes, had not wandered all over the European continent searching for a home. They had settled in central and northern Gaul, and allied themselves with Rome. When Clovis took the throne, he set out to conquer the surrounding territories and tribes. He was successful, and his kingdom became the basis of modern France, which takes its name from the Franks, Clovis' tribe.

A CHRISTIAN KING

Clovis' most important contribution to the future of his people, and to Western Europe, was

his conversion from German paganism to Christianity. By committing himself and his subjects to the Christian faith, he gained the support of the large Christian population of the entire West. Moreover, he gained the support of the Church fathers in Gaul.

THE HAMMER

The Church and the pope were the links to the culture and civilization of the ancient world. The Church fathers preserved the books and records of the past; they also copied them by hand, illustrating them with beautiful and elaborate designs. Church and monasteries became centers of learning, and people looked to the clergy for decisions in all kinds of matters. Kings depended on them for help and advice in government. Few kings of the Dark Ages could read and write; a ruler might give an order, but he needed a scholarly monk or priest to write it down so that it would become law.

The Church continued to support the descendants of Clovis, although they were weak and cruel and accomplished little. In later years, the Merovingian kings became mere figureheads, and the real ruler of the Franks was called the "Mayor of the Palace." The most powerful Mayor of the Palace was Charles Martel, who was nicknamed "The Hammer" because of his strength in battle. He tried to unite all the Frankish nobles under one head, but they resisted. Each chief was jealous of his own territory and his own power. The pope and the Church supported Charles, as they did his son, Pepin, who was called Pepin the Short. Pepin gained the crown his father had never been able to win. In 752, at Soissons, he was chosen king of all the Franks. He was the first western king to be anointed by a pope, and the true founder of the Carolingian dynasty, named for his father, Charles. But it was Pepin's son Charlemagne, who would emerge as the greatest leader of the West since Julius Caesar. He was to push back the shadows of the Dark Ages and usher in a new era of civilization.

446

When the devotions came to an end, the tall man started to rise. At that moment, Pope Leo III, splended in his gold-encrusted vestments, stepped forward quickly. Placing a gold crown on the tall man's head, the pope said in a loud voice, "To Charles Augustus, crowned of God, great and pacific emperor of the Romans—life and victory!" The crowd in the cathedral cheered, just as Roman crowds had cheered so many times in the past at the coronations of the Caesars.

The new emperor was no Caesar; in fact, he was not even a Roman. He was a German, and the king of the Franks. His name was Charles, and at the time of his coronation he was called Charlemagne, which meant "Charles the Great" in French. Charlemagne was born in the year 742, the eldest son of Pepin the Short and the grandson of Charles Martel. In 752, when Charlemagne was ten years old, his father became king of the Franks. Charlemagne and his younger brother, Carloman, were proclaimed King Pepin's rightful heirs, and after Pepin died in 768, his realm was divided between them.

Charles, Called the Great

771-814

IT WAS COLD INSIDE the great cathedral of St. Peter in Rome on Christmas day, in the year 800. The breath of the closely packed worshipers rose like steam. Although their heads were bowed in prayer, many of the worshipers stole a quick glance at the man kneeling near the high altar. He was tall and heavy, with fair hair and a flowing mustache; he was dressed in a simple tunic and a fur-trimmed cloak.

CHARLEMAGNE WAS CROWNED EMPEROR OF THE ROMANS BY POPE LEO III.

Carloman died three years later, and Charlemagne was sole ruler of the Franks.

He immediately began the first of the many wars that marked his reign. Altogether, he conducted fifty-four campaigns—against the Lombards, the Saxons, the Frisians and Danes, the Avars, the Slavs, the Gascons, and the Moslems in Spain and southern Italy. Charlemagne waged so many wars that a chronicler was careful to point out that the year 790 was exceptional. "This was a year," the chronicler wrote, *"without* war." Charlemagne made war for several purposes: to extend or defend his lands, and to convert the heathen to Christianity.

CHARLEMAGNE'S WARS

For his first campaign, against the Lombards in northern Italy, Charlemagne had a perfect excuse. The king of the Lombards had attacked some cities which were held by the pope, even threatening Rome itself. Pope Hadrian appealed to Charlemagne for help. The pope reminded him that King Pepin, Charlemagne's father, had pledged eternal loyalty to the Church and the pope, promising to protect them against all en-emies. Charles answered Hadrian's appeal by crossing the Alps and attacking Lombardy. The Lombard army, outmatched by Charlemagne's well-disciplined troops, retreated behind the stone walls of their capital, Pavia. Charlemagne besieged Pavia for nine months until the Lombards were starved into surrender. While the siege was still going on, Charlemagne made an Easter pilgrimage to Rome, becoming the first Frankish king to enter the city. Although he received a tumultuous welcome, he went up the steps of St. Peter's like any ordinary pilgrim—on his hands and knees. At the top of the stairs, Pope Hadrian lifted him up and embraced him.

After conquering Lombardy and sending the deposed king into a monastery, Charlemagne turned his attention to Bavaria, in what is today southeastern Germany. Bavaria was ruled by warrior dukes who strongly objected to paying homage to Charlemagne as their king and overlord. They did not object for long. Charles defeated them in battle, deposed their leader, and claimed the territory as part of his empire.

One of Charlemagne's most important accomplishments was the conquest of Saxony, in east and northeast Germany. It took him twenty-three years of bloody and savage fighting to sub-

due the fierce, pagan Saxon tribes. For many years they had crossed the Frankish borders, raiding towns, plundering monasteries, and looting farms, then melting back into the countryside before they could be captured.

The Saxons worshiped trees and streams and often sacrificed human beings to their bloodthirsty gods. They were determined to remain pagan, and Charlemagne was equally determined to convert them to Christianity. Time after time he would defeat their armies, forcing the leaders to accept his authority and give hostages. He would establish garrisons and bring in missionaries. Soon after he had moved on, however, the Saxons would revolt, massacre the garrisons, and murder the missionaries. Finally Charlemagne beheaded hundreds of the Saxon leaders, deported thousands of Saxons to Frankish territory and colonized Saxon lands with his own people. He issued a stern edict that gave the Saxons their choice of accepting Christianity or death. Alcuin, the great English scholar at Charlemagne's court, bitterly criticized these harsh actions, but Charlemagne did not change his policy. He was determined to bring all of western Europe under his rule and make it obedient to the authority of the Christian church.

THE SONG OF ROLAND

Charlemagne's only real military defeat came in Spain. One of his dreams was to push the Saracens, or Moslems, in Spain farther south and convert the northern part of the country to Christianity. In 778 he led two armies over the Pyrenees Mountains. He attacked the Spanish city of Saragossa but failed to capture it. During the siege of the city, he was called home to put down one of the many Saxon revolts. He set out with the main body of his army, protected by a rear guard under the command of his friend Roland, the governor of Brittany and a fine warrior.

When Roland and his men marched through a mountain pass near Roncesvalles, they were ambushed by a Basque army. The Basques were a fiercely independent people who lived on both sides of the Pyrenees. Although badly outnumbered, Roland refused to blow a blast on his horn —the signal that would call back Charlemagne and the main body of the army. He felt it was a matter of honor for the rear guard to protect the

troops heading north. Roland's heroic battle became a legend and was the subject of a poem called *The Song of Roland,* an important work in French literature. The epic poem tells how Roland wielded his sword with superhuman strength as he and his men bravely fought the Basques. At last Roland blew a blast on his horn, summoning Charlemagne. Traitors tried to delay Charlemagne, and he hesitated. Then the horn sounded a second time, and Charlemagne rushed to the rescue—but it was too late. Roland lay dead, and the Basques had escaped.

THE SPANISH MARCH

Years later, Charlemagne returned to Spain and established a powerful military base, known as the Spanish March. This was one of many military "marches" that formed a ring around the borders of Charlemagne's empire. With the defeat of the Avars, who lived east of the Danube River, and the Czechs and the Danes, who lived in northern Europe, Charlemagne dominated almost the whole of Europe. Except for the Scandinavians far to the north, and the Angles and Saxons who had managed to escape to Britain, Charlemagne had brought all the Germanic peoples into one united nation. When he was crowned by Pope Leo III in 800, he became the emperor of what would later be called the Holy Roman Empire.

But Charlemagne was more than a conqueror; he was a wise and just ruler. He set up a system of relief for the poor, supporting it with taxes paid by the nobles and the clergy. Unlike earlier warrior kings, he valued culture and learning. He was particularly interested in education. He encouraged churches and monasteries to set up schools, and told the directors to "take care to make no difference between the sons of serfs and of freemen, so that they might come and sit on the same benches to study grammar, music, and arithmetic," although he himself did not learn to read or write until late in life. His secretary noted that Charlemagne "used to keep tablets under his pillow in order that at leisure hours he might accustom his hand to form the letters; but as he began these efforts so late in life, they met with ill success."

Charlemagne welcomed scholars from everywhere in Europe, putting some of them to work at translating old texts and copying manuscripts. He brought in books from other countries and set up a school of his own. He attended the school himself, along with his wife, his sons, his daughters, and his secretary. The palace school, as it was known, was open to the children of government officials and nobles, and to any other promising children brought to Charlemagne's attention.

A devout Christian, Charlemagne took a deep interest in the Church. He kept a sharp eye on the clergy. He expected them to be faithful, dedicated men, following the strict rules laid down by Pope Gregory I and St. Benedict, the founder of the order of Benedictine monks.

Charlemagne issued many laws for the Church —laws concerning property, buildings, discipline, education, and ritual. To make sure his wishes were carried out, he sent *missi dominici,* or royal messengers, throughout the land. They reported directly to him everything they saw and heard. According to ancient records, Charlemagne ordered his royal messengers "to investigate and to report any inequality or injustice . . . to render justice to all, to the holy churches of God, to the poor, to widows and orphans and to the whole people." He also warned them "not to be hindered in the doing of justice by the flattery or bribery of anyone, by their partiality for their

MAP SHOWS THE DIVISION OF CHARLEMAGNE'S EMPIRE INTO THREE KINGDOMS. BELOW, CHARLES OF THE WEST FRANKS RECEIVES A BOOK FROM THE CHURCH.

LOTHAIR CLAIMED THE TITLE OF EMPEROR.

own friends or by the fear of powerful men."

In contrast to later kings, who would govern from a palace in a capital city, Charlemagne had no formal capital. He was constantly on the move. When he was not on a military campaign, he traveled from one royal estate to another. With him moved his court, made up of hundreds of people—courtiers, advisers, soldiers, scholars, clerks, clergy, cooks, and servants. Wherever they went, they had to have food and shelter. This was something of a problem, for there were no public accommodations, and towns were far apart. Although Charlemagne owned lands in many parts of his kingdom, often he and his court would stay with one of his vassals—the noblemen who had sworn an oath of loyalty to

him. Such a visit was a great honor, but sometimes the expense of putting up so many people left the honored nobleman close to bankruptcy.

LORDS AND SERFS

Wealth in Charlemagne's time was drawn almost completely from the land. The king and the nobles controlled vast estates, much as they had in the last days of the Roman Empire. Part of the estate was set aside for the use of the lord; part was farmed by tenants. These tenants called themselves freemen, but they were little better off than the serfs, for they had to serve both their lord and the king. They were required to work the lord's fields, to make certain payments of money to him, and to do various other services for him. In addition, they could be called up at any time to fight in the king's army. To escape so crushing a burden, many freemen voluntarily became serfs. In this way, society began to move toward the system that would become known as feudalism.

Without realizing it, Charlemagne himself helped to break down the unity he had so carefully built up. It was his practice to reward his loyal followers by giving them lands worked by serfs. These followers became lords of their own lands and could do what they pleased with them; often they gave some of their lands and serfs as a reward to their own followers. While Charlemagne lived, it seemed as though his empire would endure for ages, but within a few years after his death in 814, it began to fall apart.

Charlemagne's power passed to his son, Louis the Pious, who brought back an old custom and divided his empire among his three sons. Each of them was dissatisfied with his portion, and they promptly began quarreling among themselves. The eldest, Lothair, revolted against his father and for a time deposed him. When Louis died, the two younger brothers, Ludwig and Charles, allied themselves against Lothair, who claimed the title of emperor.

After two years of warfare, the brothers negotiated a peace and signed the Treaty of Verdun. Lothair was given the title of emperor and a kingdom carved out of the middle of the empire; it included Rome and the northern half of Italy. Ludwig received the region to the east, called the East-Frankish kingdom. Charles received the region to the west, called the West-Frankish kingdom. The East-Frankish kingdom would many centuries later become the nation called Germany the West-Frankish kingdom the nation called France; the middle kingdom would remain a troubled area and be fought over for centuries to come.

With the Treaty of Verdun, Charlemagne's great empire came to an end; ended, too, was any hope for a united Europe. Once again Europe was a divided land.

Fury From the North
814-1042

". . . FROM THE FURY OF THE NORTHMEN, Good Lord, deliver us." Until recent times, this line was included in the prayer book used by the Church of England. The raids of the Norse Vikings on Britain were so terrible that the victims never forgot them. For generations the memory of the savage Norsemen was kept alive, and Englishmen repeated this prayer for more than a thousand years. And it was not only Britain that felt the fury of the Norsemen; they raided the European continent as well.

The Norsemen's ships themselves seemed to threaten terror. The hull of a Viking ship was long and narrow, bristling with sweeping oars and studded with round, brightly painted shields. The square sail was painted with colored stripes, and the towering bow was carved into a dragon's head. And when the ships reached shore, their threat of terror proved to be no empty one. A swarm of blond, heavily bearded warriors leaped from the decks and stormed inland, looting, burning, killing. A French chronicler, writing of the Viking invasions, said, "They destroyed houses, and razed monasteries and churches to the ground, and brought to their death the servants of our holy religion by famine and sword, or sold them beyond the sea. They killed the dwellers in the land and none could resist them. . . . The Northmen ceased not to take Christian people captive and to kill them, and to destroy churches and

houses and burn villages. Through the streets lay bodies of the clergy, of laymen, nobles, and others, of women, children, and suckling babes. There was no road nor place where the dead did not lie; and all who saw Christian people slaughtered were filled with sorrow and despair."

The Norsemen, or Northmen, came from the Scandinavian lands which would later be known as Denmark, Norway, and Sweden. Whenever they set out in search of trade or booty, they said, in their own language, that they were "going a-viking"—and so they were called Vikings. Until the ninth century, when the Viking fleets began to appear on the shores of southern Europe, Scandinavia was an almost unknown country. The Vikings were still pagan when the rest of Europe was Christian. They were brutal and primitive, but they were masters of shipbuilding and sailing.

Although small parties of Norse traders had been sailing south for years, the Viking invasions of Britain, Ireland, and Europe began shortly after the death of Charlemagne in 814. Within the next 200 years, the Vikings helped to speed the collapse of the Carolingian empire, established a kingdom in Ireland, conquered part of England and France, founded colonies in Russia, settled Iceland, and discovered Greenland and the North American continent. For the Vikings were more than plunderers and pirates; they were eager for trade.

Sometimes, too, they hoped to escape political oppression in Scandinavia and find new homes. In 872, a Norse warrior named Harold Fairhaired won a great tribal battle and declared himself King of Norway. Many of the defeated clan chiefs, called "jarls," set out for foreign lands with their tribes. When they arrived, they established new homes in the only way they knew—by conquering the local inhabitants, taking over their territory, and setting up their own communities.

THE VIKINGS

Among the lands which suffered most from the Viking invasions were Ireland, Britain, and France. For centuries Ireland had been ruled by petty kings, or clan chiefs, who governed their people and a certain portion of land. The island had been converted to Christianity about the year 400, by a young Briton known to history as Saint

Patrick. The Christian faith had a great effect on the Irish. Many monasteries and churches sprang up and Irish scholars and missionaries became respected throughout Europe. The Vikings almost destroyed Irish culture. They remained a destructive force until 1014, when they were defeated by the Irish chieftain Brian of Munster at Dublin.

It is likely that the Vikings first learned of Iceland from the Irish monks who had visited Iceland as missionaries. The Norse colonization began in 874, after Igolf Arnarson was driven out of Norway and began seeking a new homeland. The colony grew rapidly, and in the year 1000 it adopted Christianity. The Vikings of Iceland produced a remarkable literature. In epic poems, called "sagas," they preserved the old Norse traditions and the stories of the pagan gods.

The Vikings had struck out for Iceland after invading Ireland; from Iceland they pushed farther west to Greenland. There Eric the Red founded a colony in 986. His son, Leif Erikson, decided to sail still farther west, across the Atlantic Ocean, to see what lay beyond the sea. The voyage was long and dangerous, for the Vikings navigated by dead reckoning—by observing the position of the sun and the stars. Even so, Lief and his crew discovered and explored the northeast coast of North America. They failed in their attempt to plant a colony, but ancient Norse writings mention the new lands of Markland, Hulluland, and Vinland. These regions are probably what today are known as Nova Scotia, Newfoundland, and Cape Cod.

Viking attacks along the northeastern coast of Britain began in the late 700's. They continued for 150 years, until finally a Danish king sat on the English throne. When the first Danish Vikings invaded Britain, the land was divided into several small kingdoms under weak kings. No one could stop the savage Danes, and they overran the whole of eastern England, taking the cities of Canterbury, London, Surrey, and York. "The Danes got the victory," wrote one chronicler, "and slew the king, and subdued all· the land and destroyed all the churches and monasteries."

The Danes met little opposition in Britain until 871. That year King Alfred the Great of Wessex, the West-Saxon kingdom, succeeded in uniting his people and stopping the advancing Danes.

Alfred was unable to push them out of Britain altogether, so he signed a treaty giving them a large portion of eastern England, which became known as the Danelaw. The Danelaw became practically a Danish nation on English soil, but it kept the Danes confined within a certain area and prevented them from spreading into the rest of Britain.

THE VIKING CONQUESTS

Alfred was still not satisfied. He set out to win back the Danelaw, setting up large forts on the lands he took. What Alfred began, King Athelstan finished, and by 940 all of the Danelaw was in English hands. For some years there was peace—a peace that was broken in 980 by a second Danish invasion, led by King Sven Forkedbeard. The English king at that time was Athelred, and he decided that he could not fight off the Danes. Instead, he paid them to stay out of England. The payment was called Danegeld, and now, of course, the Danes had a perfect excuse to return—to collect the Danegeld. They did return from year to year, and if the English did not pay, the Danes raided them. Finally, in 1016, Sven's son, Canute, seized the English throne. He was the King Canute who, according to legend, sat on a beach and commanded the tide of the ocean to stop rolling in. The waves kept coming, and Canute got his feet thoroughly wet.

In spite of his experience with the tide, Canute was a strong and powerful king. His two sons, who ruled after him, were not nearly so powerful, and in 1042 a descendant of Alfred the Great took the throne. His name was Edward the Confessor, and he would be remembered as the founder of Westminster Abbey, the great cathedral which became the final resting place for kings and queens and other notable persons.

To the Vikings, the coastline of western Europe, broken by many wide, navigable rivers, was an invitation to invade the former empire of Charlemagne. They went up the Somme, the Seine, the Rhine, and the Loire rivers into the heart of the European continent. From France they moved on to the coasts of Spain and Italy.

THE LONGBOAT OF A GREAT VIKING CHIEF WAS USED FOR HIS FUNERAL PYRE.

455

THE VIKING INVADERS TRIED FOR TEN MONTHS TO CAPTURE OR STARVE PARIS.

Charlemagne's empire had been divided into three kingdoms, each ruled by one of his grandsons, and this gave the Vikings a great advantage. The three kings were weak and had no talent for warfare. Furthermore, the nobles, who wanted to gain power for themselves, refused to support the kings for fear of strengthening the monarchs' power. And the common people allied themselves to various nobles, who could protect them. The result was that there was no military force strong enough to oust the Vikings, and the French, like the English, paid Danegeld to buy off the invaders.

During the ninth and the tenth centuries, Frankish kings paid out huge sums to the Norse chieftains. But buying off one group of invaders was no guarantee against invasions by other groups. Sailing up the Seine River, the Norsemen attacked Paris in 845, in 851, and in 861. In 885, they tried again, with an amazingly large force—40,000 men and 700 vessels. The Parisians fought back. For ten months the people of the besieged city held out, under the inspired leadership of Gozelin, the bishop of Paris, and Odo, the count of Paris. Food became scarce, and to keep from starving, the Parisians ate roots,

tic to the Black Sea and the trading centers of Constantinople and Baghdad, came to be known as the Varangian Route. In 862 the Swedish chieftain Rurik founded a Viking state near Novgorod which became the basis of the Russian monarchy.

ARABS AND MAGYARS

The Vikings were not the only invaders of Europe. From North Africa, Crete, and southern Spain came the Moslems, whom the Europeans called Saracens. Followers of Mohammed, they believed that a sure way to attain Paradise was to slaughter non-believers. They poured into southern France and Italy, but in 849, when they were almost at the gates of Rome, they were turned back by troops under Pope Leo IV. No one, however, could dislodge them from Sicily, the island at the tip of the Italian boot. The Moslems held Sicily for two centuries, dominating the Mediterranean Sea and cutting off trade routes between western Europe and the Byzantine Empire.

Eastern Europe was threatened by a new wave of Mongolian invaders, the Magyars. Like the Huns, they were nomads, fierce fighters, and magnificent horsemen. They used the bow and arrow with deadly precision, shooting as they rode their galloping horses. They swept across the steppes of southern Russia into western Germany, and then into southern France and northern Italy. Like the Vikings before them, the Magyars collected tribute from weak kings and fearful nobles. This went on until 933, when they were defeated by a German army led by King Henry I.

After the middle of the tenth century, Europe was no longer threatened by either the Arabs or the barbarians, and could develop its own way of life. Charlemagne's former empire was now governed by weak kings who were constantly dividing and subdividing their realms into smaller and smaller portions. They were too weak to control the nobles—the powerful lords, counts, and dukes who ruled their own lands, waging their own private wars, administering justice, and coining money. The result was that the ordinary man no longer felt a tie of loyalty to his king. Instead, he pledged his allegiance to the nearest lord, who could offer him protection and the means of making a living. And so feudalism came into being; it would be a way of life and a system of government for centuries to come.

acorns, dogs, cats, and rats. Finally the Frankish king, Charles the Fat, bought off the Norsemen with gold and the promise that he would not interfere while they ravaged the province of Burgundy. This earned Charles the hatred of his subjects, and soon afterward he left France, never to return. Paris was famous throughout Europe as a brave and heroic city, and from the family of its courageous leader, the Count of Paris, would come the future kings of France.

After their failure to take Paris, the Norsemen became interested in establishing a permanent home for themselves in France. They had settled in large numbers along the coast opposite England, and in 911 they signed a treaty with Charles the Simple of France giving them this land for their own. At first known as the Norselaw, the region was later called Normandy and its inhabitants Normans. Their duke, Hrolf, agreed to be a vassal of King Charles, and within a hundred years the Normans became staunch Christians and adopted the language, customs, and manners of France. A few decades later, the Norman conquest of England would change the whole pattern of life in the British Isles and have a great influence on western civilization.

While the Danes and the Norsemen were overrunning western Europe, the Swedish Vikings crossed the Baltic Sea and moved along the rivers toward the interior of Russia. Here they founded settlements and began trading with the Slavs. The Slavs called the newcomers Varangians, and the great water route they established, from the Bal-

457

The Castle and
the Manor

900-1300

COUNT LEON, lord of the vast domain of Grand-pré, stirred and waved away his servants. As he opened his eyes, the first rays of the sun were slanting through the narrow windows of his bedchamber. He stared sleepily at the tapestry hanging on the thick stone wall. It depicted a stag hunt, and he enjoyed looking at it, for there were few things in the world he loved more than hunting. For a few minutes he lay there, listening to the sounds drifting up from the courtyard —the clop of horses' hoofs, the creak of leather, the clatter of boots on cobblestones. The castle was coming awake.

Some of the count's people would be going to the fields that lay beyond the castle walls and the moat. As far as the eye could see, the land belonged to Count Leon. And, although this castle was his principal residence, he had other holdings as well—manors and manor houses, farmlands and forests. It did not occur to the count to feel grateful for his wealth and position and power. After all, they were his right; he had inherited them from his father, who had in turn inherited them from *his* father, who been granted the land as a fief by the king.

Getting up from his massive bed, Count Leon began to dress, not bothering to call his servants to attend him. He put on a short shirt over the white linen undergarments he wore even when he slept. He pulled long hose up over his legs, then slipped a tunic over his head and belted it at the waist. Finally, he thrust his feet into soft boots, combed his shoulder-length hair with his fingers, and went out the door. The count's clothes were little different from those worn by the other people of the castle, except that they were made of finer materials. But only persons of noble birth were permitted to have fur on their garments, and when the count presided at his court of justice, he would put on a long fur-trimmed robe.

As usual, Count Leon began his day by attending mass with members of his family and household. His private chapel was near the castle's huge stone tower, which was called a "donjon" or "keep." The service was followed by a light breakfast of bread and wine. After eating, the count set out on a tour of inspection; unlike some feudal lords, he was a competent and careful administrator.

THE LORD AND THE VASSAL

Crossing the bailey, or open courtyard of the castle, the count saw Sir Robert Dubois, one of his vassals. Sir Robert had inherited the fief of Dubois on the recent death of his father. For several generations the Dubois family had held its fief as a grant from the great lords of Grand-pré. It consisted of a manor house, three villages, and some three hundred acres of farm and forest land. Each time the fief holder of Dubois died, his heir was required to renew the oath of fealty, or faithfulness, to his liege lord, or suzerain. It was to make this public vow of faithfulness, known as homage, that Sir Robert had come to the castle. In return, Count Leon would swear to protect him, to give him military aid when needed, to right his wrongs, and to guard and protect his children. If Sir Robert's father had left no children, the Dubois fief would have reverted back to Count Leon, who could have turned it over to another vassal. If Sir Robert's father had left only a daughter, Count Leon would have arranged a marriage for her and the fief would have been her dowry.

Like any vassal who had been granted a fief, Sir Robert owed definite services to his lord. He would have to attend Count Leon at the count's court, assist in administering justice, and contribute money when requested. He was required to answer a summons to battle, bringing with him a certain number of fighting men, decided by contract. And whenever the count traveled across the Dubois lands, Sir Robert would be ex-

A TYPICAL FORTIFIED CASTLE OF THE MEDIEVAL PERIOD. THE TALL SQUARE TOWER AT TOP LEFT IS THE DONJON OR KEEP, AN INNER FORTRESS TO WHICH THE LORD AND HIS SUPPORTERS COULD RETREAT IF ATTACKERS SUCCEEDED IN GETTING THROUGH THE OUTER DEFENSES.

HUNTERS AND FARMERS OF THE MIDDLE AGES USED PRIMITIVE
SPEARS AND OX-DRAWN PLOWS IN THEIR OCCUPATIONS.

pected to feed and house the count and all his company.

This intricate kind of private government, known as feudalism, was for hundreds of years the political system of western Europe and England. Powerful nobles held the rights and privileges which had formerly been held only by strong kings, such as Charlemagne. A poet, mourning the death of Charlemagne, wrote:

> *Once we had a king,*
> *Now we have kinglets.*
> *Once we had an empire—*
> *Now only fragments called kingdoms.*

The unit of government was no longer even a kingdom, but the domain of the feudal lord, who administered justice, settled quarrels, coined his own money, collected tolls from roads and bridges on his land, levied taxes, and demanded military service from his vassals. In theory, a feudal lord owed loyalty to his sovereign, the king; in practice, the lords did as they pleased. Most of the kings of the feudal period were little more than figureheads. Often they traveled from one castle to another, living on gifts from the mighty lords.

And so it was that Sir Robert, like all vassals, paid little attention to his distant king. He knew that the king had neither the riches nor the power

THE KNIGHTS AND NOBLES WORE EXPENSIVE SUITS OF CHAIN-
MAIL ARMOR AND HUNTED WITH FALCONS FOR SPORT.

of Count Leon, who had hundreds of vassals and could put in the field an army twice as large as any the king could raise. Sir Robert was proud to serve such a powerful lord and would gladly fight for him in wars against other lords.

THE CODE OF CHIVALRY

Now the count paused in the bailey to greet Sir Robert. Wishing to learn more about his new vassal, he invited the young man to attend him throughout the day. Sir Robert was pleased and flattered. He was eager to make a good im-

pression on his lord; besides, he was anxious to discuss the question of marriage. He wanted to marry the Lady Charlotte of Croyes, an orphan who was the count's ward. According to feudal custom, the count had the right, as Lady Charlotte's guardian, to marry her to whomever he chose.

Sir Robert stood by while Count Leon ordered a man to repair the huge windlass which raised and lowered the portcullis. The portcullis was the heavy oak and iron gate that guarded the entrance to the castle. Beyond it was a drawbridge spanning the moat, the deep, water-filled ditch around the entire enclosure of the castle. If an

It was the knight's duty to train him thoroughly in horsemanship and all the arts of war, as well as in hunting, hawking, and other sports. At twenty, a squire was ready to be accepted as a knight of the sword, whose code was "to fear God and maintain the Christian religion, to protect the weak and defenseless, to live for honor and glory, to fight for the general welfare of all . . . to respect the honor of women, to refuse no challenge from an equal and never to turn the back upon a foe." Few knights of the Middle Ages were able to live up to this ideal of chivalry, but for centuries it would remain the standard of conduct for a gentleman.

Although a squire could be knighted on the field of battle, for exceptional bravery, usually he became a knight in a religious ceremony. Robed in garments of white, red, and black, he guarded his arms all night before the altar of the church. The following morning, after mass and communion, he received the accolade of knighthood, a blow on the shoulder with the flat of a sword, from either his liege lord or a bishop.

A KNIGHT'S TRADE

Count Leon and Sir Robert watched the young squires for a few moments, and then went on to inspect the stables. Count Leon was especially proud of his charger, his huge and spirited war horse, and ordered the stable boys to bring some fresh straw for its stall. Next the two nobles went to the smithy, where they admired a new suit of armor, beautifully etched with the coat of arms of Grandpré. They also carefully examined an array of broadswords, daggers, battle-axes, and lances that had just been turned out by the smithy.

Their interest in weapons was not surprising, for making war was a knight's trade. Private wars between lords and knights, often caused by disputes over lands, were common during the Middle Ages. And yet, since only knights usually took part in the fighting, the number of persons involved was comparatively small; it was not until the late Middle Ages that battles were waged by large armies. Nor were the wars always bloody.

enemy attacked, the drawbridge could be raised, for the castle was a fort as well as the count's principal home. Besides the great donjon, there were two other towers at the angles of the encircling walls; from them the archers could shoot arrows at the attackers below. The castle could hold out against a siege of many months, for within its walls were storehouses, shops, bakeries, kitchens, artisans' dwellings, quarters for troops and guests, stables, a smithy, an armory, and a drill ground.

As Count Leon and Sir Robert made their way to the stables, they saw two young squires practicing swordsmanship on the drill ground. Sir Robert smiled, for he had put in many hours of practice on this same drill ground while receiving his own training for knighthood. It was the custom for a vassal's son to be sent to the court of a liege lord at seven years of age, to serve seven years as a page. During this period he was cared for by the women of the household, who instructed him in religion, courtesy, deportment, and cleanliness. At the age of fourteen he became a squire, a personal attendant to a knight.

Often a knight preferred to capture, rather than kill, his opponent and release him in return for a ransom.

When there were no wars to fight, knights would take part in tournaments, a favorite pastime of the nobility. These war games, held at the invitation of some noble, would take place on a field called "the lists," with barriers separating the contestants from the spectators. Tournaments usually included contests between individuals, called jousts, and group combats, and prizes were given to the victors. Although the knights used blunted lances and swords, and the object was to unhorse the opponent, the sport was rough and dangerous. Eager to make their reputations as warriors, the knights fought hard, and many were injured or killed.

And so it was that Count Leon and Sir Robert examined the weapons in the smithy carefully. They were discussing the last tournament as they entered the Great Hall of the castle for dinner. Because breakfast was so meager, the mid-day meal was served early, around ten o'clock in the morning. Noise and confusion filled the vast room as dozens of people took their places at the long trestle tables that had been set up. The count's own table stood on a dais, or platform. Lady Elaine, his wife, sat at his left; Sir Robert at his right, in the place of honor. Also at the count's table were members of his family, his squire, his priest-confessor, and important household officials. Lesser members of the household sat at the other tables, along with such visiting travelers as knights-at-arms, monks, merchants, and troubadours.

A KNIGHT'S OATH

Food was plentiful on this day, for the early spring crops were in. There were meat, fish, and pastries, as well as the vegetables known to the *Middle Ages*—cabbage, turnips, onions, carrots, beans, and peas—and freshly baked bread, cheese,

TOURNAMENTS WERE A FAVORITE PASTIME OF KNIGHTS AND NOBLES.

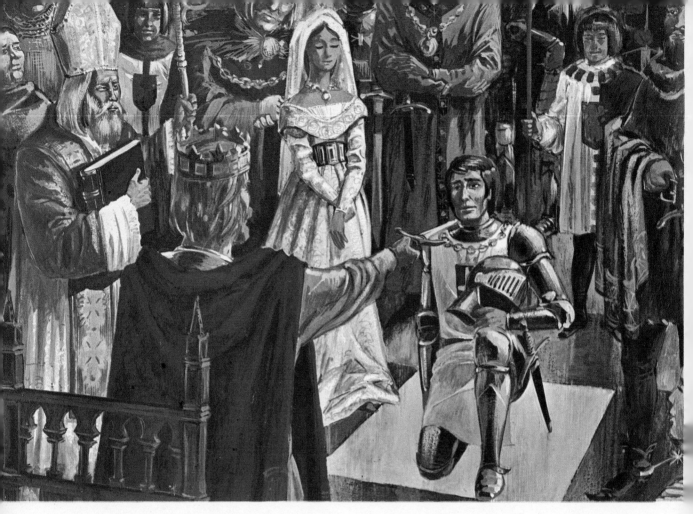

THE DUBBING OF A KNIGHT WAS ONE OF THE MOST SOLEMN FEUDAL CEREMONIES.

and early pears, all washed down with large tankards of ale or wine. Fruit juices and honey were the only sweetening. Spices were almost unknown until they were introduced from the Orient, after the Crusades. Everyone ate with his fingers, using a dagger to cut meat. Bones and refuse were thrown on the floor for the dogs.

While eating, Lady Elaine informed her husband that she would be riding over to a nearby village that was part of the original estate of Grandpré. Fever had broken out there. In an age when physicians were few, it was the duty of the lord's wife to aid the sick and poor of her husband's fief. This was only one of her many duties; she was responsible for managing every detail of the domestic arrangements of the household.

Count Leon ordered two of his knights to ride escort to his wife. Then he rose, signaling the end of the meal, and the Great Hall was prepared for the court of justice. The first business before the court was Sir Robert's act of homage and oath of fealty. Wrapping himself in his fur-trimmed robe, Count Leon seated himself on his carved chair of office, and beckoned to Sir Robert to approach. He asked the young knight if he was willing to be completely his man. "I am willing," Sir Robert answered, and, kneeling, placed his clasped hands in the hands of the count. Sir Robert swore, "I promise on my faith that I will in future be faithful to Count Leon, and will observe my homage to him completely against all persons, in good faith and without deceit."

Count Leon kissed him, raised him from his knees, and proclaimed the grant of the fief: "I Leon, count palatine of Grandpré, make known to those present and to come that I have given in fee to Robert Dubois and his heirs the manor which is called DuBois, and whatever the same Robert shall be able to acquire in the same manor I have granted to him and his heirs in augmentation of that fief. . . . The same Robert on account of this had become my liege man. . . ."

After the ceremony of homage, Count Leon

THE KNIGHT SWORE AN OATH OF LOYALTY TO HIS LORD AND BECAME HIS LIEGE MAN.

sat in judgment on various matters brought before him by his bailiff. He settled a dispute between two villeins, or peasants, over a patch of farmland. Next he heard the case of a poacher who had dared to hunt on the count's game preserve and had killed a deer. This was a serious offense, for only the nobility had the right to hunt, and the count sentenced the guilty man to have his right hand struck off at the wrist. Finally, one of the count's vassal knights was brought before the court and accused of highway robbery. His case was postponed until Count Leon could summon a group of knights to sit in judgment, for it was a rule of feudal justice that a noble must be tried by his peers, or equals.

LIFE ON THE MANOR

After the count adjourned his court, he and Sir Robert spent the afternoon hunting, with both dogs and falcons. Count Leon's prize falcon brought down three braces of doves, and Sir Robert speared a wild boar. Galloping back toward the castle, the hunting party passed a group of serfs digging channels to drain a swamp. Sir Robert asked if they might pause so that he could observe how the channels were dug. He was planning to drain some marshlands on his own fief. Count Leon agreed; the more a vassal improved his manor, the more valuable it was to his lord.

Feudal society, which was based on agriculture, could not have existed without manorialism, as the economic system of the Middle Ages was called. The wealth of the nobles came from the manorial lands, which were worked by the peasants and the serfs. Some lords owned only one manor, but the great lords, like Count Leon, owned many. A manor consisted of a manor house, a village or villages, and perhaps several thousand acres of meadow, pasture, woodland, and cultivated land. The cultivated land was divided into small strips, with about a third of the strips reserved for the lord and a smaller part for the Church. The remaining strips were assigned to the peasants and serfs for their use.

For at least half of each week, peasants and serfs worked the land belonging to the lord and the Church. They also had to do "boon work," such as hauling, harvesting, cutting firewood, and building roads and bridges. The rest of the time they cared for their own strips of land.

The serfs enjoyed even less freedom than the peasants. A serf was the chattel, or property, of his lord, and was bound to the land for life, as were his children and his children's children. He was permitted to own no property and he could not marry without his lord's permission. And yet a serf was not a slave; feudal law gave him certain rights and defined the lord's duties toward him. If a manor was sold or given as a fief to a vassal or another lord, the serf was not displaced; he remained with the land. He was entitled to military protection by his lord and was exempt from military service.

A manor was a self-contained unit which produced all of its necessities. It had its own craftsmen, such as weavers, tanners, carpenters, blacksmiths, and millers. Life on a manor centered around the village, which might be populated by only a dozen families or as many as fifty or sixty. Peasants and serfs lived in hovels that had dirt floors and no windows or chimneys. The furnishings were few and simple—three-legged stools, a trestle table, and beds that were boxes on the floor, filled with straw or dry leaves. Unlike the nobles, peasants and serfs rarely ate meat. They ate mostly porridge, cheese, black bread, and whatever vegetables they could grow themselves.

THE THREE ESTATES

The life of the peasant was hard and monotonous. An early Anglo-Saxon writer quotes a peasant as saying, "Oh, sir, I work very hard. I go out in the dawning, driving the oxen to the field and I yoke them to the plough. Be the winter never so stark, I dare not stay home for fear of my lord; but every day I must plough a full acre or more. . . . Yes, indeed it is very hard work." But a peasant had his pleasures, too. He did not work on Sundays, nor on saints' days, which came frequently. He might visit a nearby market or fair, where he would mingle with the crowds

CROWDS FLOCKED TO THE FAIRS FOR A DAY OF TRADE AND AMUSEMENT.

and watch a conjuror or a strolling band of acro-bats. He enjoyed village dances and harvest and vintage festivals, and sometimes the lord of the manor would give a feast to celebrate a wedding or a christening or the completion of the spring sowing.

Peasant or noble, priest or lord—each man had his place in society. Each man was a member of one of three estates, or classes, and was expected to carry out the duties of his estate. The first estate was the clergy, who were responsible for the Church and religion. The second estate was

467

the nobility, whose duty it was to govern. All other men were part of the third estate, and it was their duty to work, to produce food and all the other necessities of life.

EACH MAN IN HIS PLACE

Neither Count Leon nor Sir Robert ever doubted that this was the way things were meant to be. God had put each man in his place, high or low, and who could question God's wisdom? This was the way the world was, and so it would continue to be until the end of time. Seated on their horses that day, looking down at the peasants digging ditches, pleasantly tired after the hunt, Count Leon and Sir Robert felt that all was right with the world. They were in the best of humor as they made their way to the castle for the evening meal, which would be served at sundown.

Some travelers had arrived during the afternoon—a bishop returning to his cathedral, a merchant from the Republic of Venice, a knight on a mission, and a wandering troubadour. The count made them all welcome; Lady Elaine had already assigned them sleeping quarters and given orders for a lavish banquet. When Count Leon and his guests sat down at the tables in the Great Hall, the servants brought in huge pastries and meat pies, and spitted boar and roast swan and peacock. There was wine during the meal, and even more afterward, when the troubadour entertained the company with *chansons de gestes,* or songs of deeds, and *chansons d'amour,* or love songs.

Sir Robert chose this moment to ask the count for the hand of Lady Charlotte of Croyes. Count Leon was pleased that the fief of Sir Robert would be joined to that of Lady Charlotte; the young man would manage them well. He quickly gave his assent to the marriage, then proposed a toast to the betrothal of his liege man, Sir Robert, to his ward, the Lady Charlotte. Sir Robert in turn toasted his liege lord, Count Leon, to whom he pledged his loyalty and his strong right arm, in peace and war. Still more toasts were drunk, and the great hall of the castle was filled with singing and merriment. But the hour was growing late, and at last the count pushed himself away from the table and started for his chamber and bed. The others followed his example, and a day at the castle of Grandpré—a typical day in the life of the Middle Ages—came to an end.

Feudal Germany
936-1250

THE WINTER of 1077 was one of the coldest on record in Italy. Ice and snow choked the mountain passages in the north, and snowdrifts were piled high well into the south—as far south as the castle of Canossa, which was southeast of Parma. The fortified castle belonged to the countess of Tuscany, and here Pope Gregory VII had taken refuge, fearing an attack by his enemies. On January 25, a man stood outside the castle gate, barefoot in spite of the snow and

EMPEROR HENRY IV WALKED THROUGH THE SNOW AT CANOSSA TO PLEAD
WITH THE POPE TO FORGIVE HIM AND LIFT HIS EXCOMMUNICATION.

cold. He was no ordinary penitent come to ask forgiveness of the pope. He was Henry IV of Germany, emperor of the Holy Roman Empire. He had made a long and perilous journey with his wife, his young son, and a few followers.

For three days the emperor waited for the pope to pardon him and lift the ban of excommunication. Excommunication was banishment from the Church, and was the most terrible punishment that could be given to a believer of the Middle Ages. Excommunication meant that he was deprived of all the privileges of a Christian. He could not attend church services, he was denied the sacraments, he could not be buried in consecrated ground. In excommunicating Henry, Pope Gregory hoped to force him to acknowledge the pope's authority to appoint his own bishops.

Henry knew that until the ban of excommunication was lifted his nobles would not accept him as king; he had little choice but to humiliate himself. Pope Gregory, for his part, knew that Henry would be a dangerous opponent once he was restored to the throne. But Gregory, too, had little choice; it was his Christian duty to take back into the Church anyone who begged so humbly for forgiveness. As Gregory later wrote, Henry "came in person to Canossa . . . bringing with him only a small retinue . . . He presented himself at the gate of the castle, barefoot and clad only in wretched woolen garments, beseeching us with fears to grant him absolution and forgiveness. This he continued to do for three days, while all those about us were moved to compassion at his plight, and interceded for him with tears and

MONKS HELPED THE CHURCH IN ITS STRUGGLE AGAINST THE NOBLES.

prayers. . . . At length we removed the excommunication from him, and received him again into the bosom of Holy Mother Church."

The king's pilgrimage to Canossa seemed like a triumph for the pope. But once he had been accepted back in the Church, Henry was able to return to his court and rally the nobles around him, and in the end the victory was his.

THE HOLY ROMAN EMPIRE

The conflict between Henry and Gregory was part of a long struggle for power between the German monarchs and the papacy. The struggle began with Otto I—and yet, when Otto took the German throne in 936, he allied himself with the bishops and archbishops of the Church. Up to this time, the German kings had been as weak as the kings of France and England. They could not control the nobles, the powerful feudal dukes and princes who ruled their domains with a strong hand. Otto, who became known as Otto the Great, saw that the monarchy needed a strong, unified state. In such a state the nobles would be loyal vassals of the king, their lands would be royal fiefs, and everyone would owe allegiance

and service to the crown. And as his first step in controlling the nobles, Otto allied himself with the Church.

The Church was willing to cooperate with Otto in order to improve its own position. In return for its support, it received grants for crown lands, special immunities, and sovereign rights, such as the right to hold court, coin money, and levy tolls. Church officials even gave Otto military aid, in exchange for the many benefits Otto gave them. Slowly, Otto made the churchmen his vassals, whom he appointed and controlled. In this way he laid the foundations of the strength which made Germany the mightest state in Europe in the tenth, eleventh, and twelfth centuries.

After his alliance with the Church was cemented, Otto secured his eastern borders by sweeping victories over the Slavs and the Magyars. He then turned toward Italy. His aim was to forge one great European state—a Holy Roman Empire which would bring back the glory of ancient Rome, but with the cooperation of the Church. He married the beautiful widow Adelheid, whose husband had been a contender for the Italian throne, declared himself king of the Lombards in north Italy, and, entering Rome on January 31, 962, had himself crowned Holy Roman Emperor. As emperor, he tried to control the pope, and when this did not work out to his satisfaction he tried to set up his own man in place of the pope.

The kings who followed Otto continued to carry out his policy of unification. Henry II, last of the line of Saxon kings, was succeeded by Conrad II of the Salian dynasty. Conrad put into action a clever plan. Whenever a dukedom fell vacant, instead of giving it to another noble, he bestowed it on his son and heir, Henry III. The result was that when Henry III took the throne in 1039, he was the duke of every German duchy except Lorraine and Saxony.

But while the German kings were building a strong state and restoring the tradition of the Holy Roman Empire, a movement sprang up that would bring the Church into direct conflict with the monarchy. This movement originated in the famous monastery of Cluny in France, and it was therefore known as the Cluniac program. The Cluniacs disapproved of the clergy becoming vassals to kings. Appealing to the pope, they called for many reforms. The pope was only too willing to support any movement that would free him from the dominance of the German kings and make him independent.

The conflict between church and state worsened during the reign of Henry III, who deposed three popes and created a succession of five German popes. His son, Henry IV, inherited the conflict and a formidable opponent as well, the autocratic and reform-minded Pope Gregory VII. Gregory had dedicated himself to the task of freeing the Church from German control. Henry finally reached the point where he declared Gregory an untrue pope, threatened to remove him from office, and ordered his German bishops to denounce him. Pope Gregory's answer was to excommunicate Henry from the Church—and it was then that Henry made his famous pilgrimage to Canossa.

The world marvelled at a penitent emperor standing barefoot in the snow and pleading with the pope, but after lifting the ban of excommunication from Henry, Gregory supported Duke Rudolph of Swabia, who revolted against the emperor. The enraged Henry returned to Italy, but this time he did not come as a humble penitent. He came as a warrior, and he brought an army with him. He fought his way to the gates of Rome and drove out Gregory, who fled for his life and died in exile. Henry replaced him with a rival pope—

A MOVEMENT TO REFORM THE CHURCH WAS STARTED AT THE MONASTERY OF CLUNY.

this time a pope who would obey the orders of the German emperor.

The struggle between the German kings and the popes went on until 1122, when the German princes met with papal delegates and members of the clergy in the city of Worms. They reached a compromise and drew up an agreement called the Concordat of Worms. It was signed by Henry IV's son, King Henry V. The Concordat gave the Church the right to name its own bishops and archbishops, although the king kept the right to invest them with their lands and fiefs. It gave the pope more control over the clergy, and so it was considered a defeat for the German kings.

The next few German emperors did little to

challenge the pope, and then, in 1152, Frederick I of the Hohenstaufen dynasty came to the throne. He was a hearty, jolly man with great strength and an enormous appetite, and his full red beard won him the name of Barbarossa, or Red-beard. The greatest German emperor of the twelfth century, he immediately set out to regain the power of the monarchy. His aims were the same as those of German kings in the past—to control the nobles, to make the bishops loyal to the king rather than to the pope, and to extend German holdings in Italy and thus create a true Holy Roman Empire. He had to fight five separate Italian campaigns, but in the end he was victorious. The Lombard League, a union of independent cities in northern Italy, signed a treaty recognizing him as overlord. After that, Barbarossa married his son and heir, Henry, to Constance, heiress to the throne of the old Norman kings in southern Italy and Sicily. Through this marriage, southern Italy and Sicily were added to the lands of the empire.

Whatever Barbarossa did, he did in a grand and lavish manner. In 1184 he called a great gathering of German princes to Mainz to celebrate the knighting of his two oldest sons. Thousands of knights and nobles traveled to Mainz, coming from every important state in Europe. A special banquet hall was built for the occasion, and two large warehouses were stocked with chickens, ducks, geese, deer, wild boar, and huge barrels of Rhine wine. After the feasting, there was a tournament, in which the sixty-year-old emperor himself took an active part, while minstrels and troubadours sang his praises.

Four years later, Barbarossa joined England's King Richard I in the Third Crusade. He never returned; he died while bathing in a river in Asia Minor. But the German people could not give up their red-bearded king so easily. A legend about him slowly grew, and it would be told as late as the nineteenth century. Frederick Barbarossa was not dead. He was only asleep somewhere high in the mountains, under a magic spell. Some day he would awake and bring back the glory of Germany.

But when Barbarossa died, Germany was still glorious. His son, Henry VI, inherited an empire at the height of its power. King of Germany and emperor of Rome, Henry was also crowned king of Sicily, Apulia, and Calabria on Christmas Day of 1194. To make sure that his own son

would succeed him, Henry had the child crowned king of the Romans at the age of two. The next year Henry died, leaving three-year-old Frederick II heir to the mightiest state in Europe.

Frederick II grew up to be the best educated and the most gifted monarch of the Middle Ages. He was called *stupor mundi,* the amazement of the world. He was a soldier, a statesman, an architect, a poet, a mathematician, a zoologist. He could speak half a dozen languages and was a patron of the arts. In spite of his brilliance, he could not hold together his empire; it was too widespread, too much of a mixture. Throughout his reign he was troubled by uncooperative German princes, by rebellious communities in northern Italy, and by an openly antagonistic pope who was determined to free Italy from German rule.

Although Frederick waged almost continuous warfare to keep his Italian lands, after his death the empire lost Sicily. Then Italy broke away, and by the middle of the thirteenth century the Holy Roman Empire which Otto the Great had founded, and which had reached its height under Barbarossa and Henry VI, was weak and almost powerless. France and England, rather than Germany, would dominate Europe.

Feudal France
814-1314

AFTER THE BREAKUP OF CHARLEMAGNE'S EM-pire, France, the western half of the empire, was ruled by a series of weak kings. They were so weak that they were known as the "do-nothing kings," and, indeed, they could do nothing to stop their powerful and greedy nobles from fighting among themselves. Finally the Carolingian line came to an end, and the Franks, as the French were then called, elected a new king. He was Hugh Capet, a relative of the famous Count Odo who had directed the defense of Paris against the Vikings.

With Hugh began the line of Capetian kings who were to rule France for many generations. The king actually held several positions. He was the sovereign of a vaguely defined nation called France; at the same time he was the fuedal lord

AN 11TH CENTURY FRENCH MANUSCRIPT
PORTRAYED THE KING ON HIS THRONE.

Ile de France, a small, compact area surrounding Paris, and it was infested by lawless vassals who terrorized the roads leading to the city. King Louis VI waged war against them. The French nicknamed him Louis the Fat, but his enormous size did not harm his ability to fight. He showed the outlaws no mercy, and, one by one, they were suppressed, exiled, or executed. Among them was Thomas of Marle, who was famous for his cruelty. Once, when a peasant told him that he was unable to walk fast, Thomas shouted, "I'll make you bestir yourself!"—and sliced off the peasant's feet with one blow of his sword.

With the Ile de France firmly under control, Louis the Fat's successor, Louis VII, began to bring vassals in other parts of the realm to justice. He summoned them to court, and if they refused to appear, he went after them with an army. Louis VII also continued Louis the Fat's policy of reorganizing the central government. The two kings discharged incompetent nobles and replaced them with men of lower birth who were loyal to the crown.

HENRY OF ANJOU

The biggest obstacle to the French kings' drive for power was the mighty duchy of Normandy on the northern coast of France. The duke of Normandy was supposed to be a vassal of the king. But in 1066, William, the duke of Normandy, crossed the English Channel with an army and conquered England. According to feudal law, the French king was still the overlord of the duke of Normandy—and the duke, by his conquest of England, was now a king in his own right.

Things grew even more complicated in 1151. By this time a young man named Henry was the duke of Normandy. The grandson of an English king, he became known as Henry of Anjou. He inherited the French duchies of Anjou, Maine, and Tourraine, and these, together with the lands he already owned, made him the lord of a vast estate, much larger than the kingdom of France.

Meanwhile, in 1137, King Louis VII had married fifteen-year-old Eleanor of Aquitaine, heiress of one of the largest and richest duchies of France. Beautiful, talented, and ambitious, Eleanor found neither her royal husband nor his

of his own lands and overlord, of suzerain, of all other French lords. He was supposed to be defender of the realm, protector of the poor, and champion of justice. But he was actually little more than a figurehead, for he had neither soldiers nor money enough to enforce his authority.

Like the German monarchs, the Capetian kings faced the problem of winning control of the powerful lords. Also like the Germans, they took the first step by establishing good relations with the Church. In their coronation oath, the French kings swore to defend the Church. And in return, for hundreds of years, the Church supported the monarchy against the feudal lords.

The hereditary fief of the French kings was the

court much to her liking. They were not lively enough for her. She once said that she thought she had married a king, but found that she had married a monk. Louis, on the other hand, was very much in love with her. He was extremely jealous—and Eleanor gave him more than one reason to be. Finally, when she was with him on the second crusade, Louis was so humiliated by her shameless conduct that he decided to divorce her. Louis got his divorce on March 21, 1152. On May 18, to Louis' surprise, Eleanor married Henry of Anjou. The following year, her new husband became king of England and was called Henry II. Almost two-thirds of France was in his hands, while Louis controlled only half of the other third.

THE CAPETIANS

Henry founded the line of English kings known as the Angevin kings, and it seemed impossible that they would not crush the Capetian kings of France. The Capetians now had less power than their former vassals. And yet for three hundred years the Capetians held on to what was theirs, and in the end they pushed the Angevins out of France. During the three-hundred-year struggle the real French nation was formed, mostly through the efforts of Louis VII's son, Philip Augustus. Philip came to the throne at the age of fourteen and reigned for forty-four years. One of the greatest of French kings, he did more than any other king before him to

strengthen the monarchy, and he laid the foundation for modern France.

Nervous, and looking anything but a hero—when he grew older he became bald and blind in one eye—Philip was patient, clever, and a master at scheming and plotting. He succeeded in winning back more than half the French territory held by the Angevin kings, a move that added immensely to France's lands and power. He managed this by supporting the rebellions of Henry's quarrelsome sons, who were constantly in conflict with their father. When the sons themselves sat on the throne, they discovered that their one-time ally and supporter was working against them.

Richard the Lion-hearted was the first of Henry's sons to become king of England. Philip joined him on a crusade to the Holy Land, but used his father-in-law's death as an excuse for returning to France. There he conspired with Richard's brother, the wily John, to attack Richard's possessions in France. Then John became king, and now Philip conspired against him, supporting the claim of John's nephew, Arthur of Brittany, to the English crown. Little by little, carefully planning and plotting, Philip extended the royal domain. The result was that the Capetians were supreme in France and their nation an important factor in the affairs of all Europe.

Philip was just as able at administering his state as he was at enlarging its territories. He appointed *bailli*, representatives of the crown who acted as both justices and sheriffs; they were much like the royal messengers appointed by Charle-

magne. Because these men were appointed and paid by the king, they did everything they could to strengthen his authority and to check the influence of the feudal lords. Philip also kept a sharp eye on his court and the royal household, making certain that his officers were men who would be loyal to him alone.

To support his administration, Philip had to find new ways to raise money. The king had no authority to levy taxes directly, but Philip got around that by imposing all sorts of special fees. Jews, for example, had to pay a special fee, as did the Italian bankers. There was a fee for liberating serfs, and once Philip tried to collect a fee from persons who did not want to go on a crusade. Communities that wanted to govern themselves as towns were required to buy charters of liberty from the crown.

Philip welcomed the rise of the towns. Not only did they provide him with money and military aid, but they were also a further check to the power of the nobles. In fact, the power of the kings might never have grown as it did without the rise of the towns; for some 600 years, or until the French Revolution, the kings looked to the townspeople for support. Philip was wise enough, too, to seek the support of the people of Paris, which had become one of the great cities of Europe. He built a twenty-eight-foot-high wall around it, improved some of the streets, gave help to the university, and began the construction of the Louvre, the palace where the French kings would live for centuries.

The kings who followed Philip continued to strengthen the monarchy and used every means to regain the French territories held by England. By the beginning of the thirteenth century, only Aquitaine, south of the Loire River, remained in English hands. Philip's son, Louis VIII, further added to the crown lands by waging war against the county of Toulouse, where a new religious movement had sprung up. The center of the movement was the diocese of Albi, and so the followers of the movement were called Albigenses. Although they were Christians, their beliefs differed from those of the Church, and the pope declared them to be heretics.

While Philip was still alive, the pope called for a war of extermination against the Albigenses; anyone who took part could seize their lands. Philip at first refused to join the nobles of the north, who were quick to take advantage of this opportunity for conquest. Later, to prevent certain nobles from becoming too powerful, he put his son Louis at the head of an army and sent them against the Albigenses. Louis was defeated, but after Philip's death, he tried again. This time the Albigenses were slaughtered and all but wiped out, and Toulouse became the property of the monarchy.

A CHRISTIAN KING

Philip's grandson, Louis IX, who took the throne in 1226, was deeply religious. He was the only monarch of the Middle Ages who tried to practice Christianity both as a king and as a man. He dressed simply, ate and drank little, and never swore or gambled. He was always concerned about the welfare of his people, particularly the poor, and he sponsored the building of countless chapels, convents, abbeys, and hospitals. He loved peace, but he loved Christianity more, and he took part in two crusades to the Holy Land. His first crusade, in 1248, ended in failure when he was captured by the Turks and forced to pay a heavy ransom. He died in 1270 while on his second crusade, and in 1297 the Church declared him a saint.

Louis IX's religious beliefs did not prevent him from being a strong ruler. His subjects could seek the king's justice at the *Parlement de Paris,* a special court where they could appeal the decisions of the feudal courts. Louis was the first French king to issue ordinances for his entire realm without first getting permission from the nobles. This was an important break with the customs of feudalism. Frenchmen began to think of themselves as subjects of the king, rather than as vassals of a lord.

PHILIP THE FAIR

Louis' son, Philip III, was weak and accomplished little in his reign of fifteen years. He was once called "the carbuncle sprung from that most precious gem of Christ, St. Louis." He died while trying to invade Aragon, and his son, Philip IV, became king. A handsome man, Philip IV was known as Philip the Fair. It was his looks, not his actions, that won him the name, for he was far different from his grandfather. He used every means he could think of to squeeze money from his complaining subjects. Commercial transactions, exemptions from military service, church property and income—all were taxed. He drove out the Jews and the Italian bankers and seized their property. He managed to get control of the vast fortune of the Knights Templar, a secret society of crusading knights who had taken religious vows. The pope declared the society heretical and its members subject to the Inquisition. Its leaders were tortured and burned at the stake.

And yet it was true that Philip the Fair had to find money to meet the needs of his rapidly expanding state, and, like the Capetian kings before him, he strengthened the monarchy. His desire for power finally led him into conflict with Pope Boniface VIII. To show the pope that all France was united behind the throne, in 1302 he called a great council of feudal nobles, knights, and representatives of towns. He consulted with them on what measures were to be used against the pope. He called two other such meetings in 1308 and 1314; they were called the Estates-General and were the closest thing to a national law-making assembly that France had known under the monarchy.

In contrast to the Holy Roman Empire, which had dissolved into a series of small states, France was growing stronger and more unified, under kings who did not hesitate to use their power and demand still more.

The Conquest of England
1066-1265

IN THE DIM LIGHT of early morning, the Frenchmen were preparing for battle. Squires helped the knights put on their armor, grooms brought up the horses, archers tested their bows, foot soldiers began to assemble, while mounted messengers hurried busily here and there. The date was October 14, 1066, and before the sun set that day a kingdom would change hands and a new era in English history would begin. The battle, one of the most decisive ever fought, would be known as the Battle of Hastings.

The cause of the battle was ambition—the driving ambition of Duke William of Normandy to win himself a kingdom and a crown. The son of a Viking pirate chief, William inherited the

French duchy of Normandy in 1035, when he was only eight years old. At the age of twenty he began to govern Normandy himself, and he proved to be a stern and able ruler. Under his firm guidance, Normandy prospered and its population increased, until William had become the French king's most powerful vassal. Unable to seek new lands and glory in France, because of his feudal oath of loyalty to the king, William decided to invade England.

Anglo-Saxon England was a loosely knit, rural land which had never really recovered from the Viking raids. The petty kingdoms ruled by

Anglo-Saxon chiefs had finally been absorbed into the Viking empire of King Canute. Then, during Edward the Confessor's reign, the country again became weak as the feudal lords struggled with each other for power. One of these lords, Harold Godwinson, seized the English crown for himself. Three weeks after Harold had taken the throne, Duke William crossed the English channel with an army of 5000 men and landed on Pevensey Beach.

Now King Harold and his hastily gathered army

VICTORY OVER KING HAROLD AT THE BATTLE OF HASTINGS GAVE WILLIAM THE CONQUERER THE ENGLISH THRONE.

had taken a position on a hill about six miles from the town of Hastings, blocking off the road to London. William had little choice but to advance against the English; behind him lay the sea. Besides, he had come to conquer and was ready to fight. He gave the signal for the attack, the trumpets sounded, and the battle began.

All day the battle went on. The French bowmen sent swarms of arrows into the enemy line, but the English troops, most of them infantrymen, stood firm. Then William ordered his horsemen into the battle. He led them himself, together with his brother Odo. Except for his bulging belly, William looked like the tough warrior he was. A chronicler described him as being "of just stature, extraordinary corpulence, fierce countenance; his forehead bare of hair; of such strength of arm that it was often a matter of surprise that no one was able to draw his bow which he him-

self could bend when his horse was on full gallop; he was majestic whether sitting or standing, although the protuberance of his belly deformed his royal person. . . ."

Suddenly the minstrel Taillefer, brandishing his sword, rode ahead of the others, straight into the midst of the English. Although he was quickly killed, his feat roused the French knights, and they, too, charged the English line. The English struck back with their heavy axes, slicing off arms and cutting down the Frenchmen's horses. William's left wing crumbled, and some of the English rushed down the hill after the fleeing men. This was a mistake. William swiftly brought his horsemen around and crushed the English who had dared to leave their places on the hill.

Even so, the English might have won the battle. But William was a master strategist; he reasoned that the enemy might make the same

The land that William had conquered had few large cities. The people were mostly farmers, and even in London, the country's largest city, the people kept cows and chickens and tended the fields. The only other cities of any size were York, to the north, and Bristol, in the western part of the country.

The entire land was divided into thirty-four regions called "shires"—a term which appears in the names of many English counties, such as Devonshire and Hampshire. Each shire was divided into smaller areas called "hundreds," which, in turn, were made up of still smaller areas known as "hides." A hide was equal to about 120 acres. A "shire court" was held twice a year, and once a month the "hundred court" met. Both courts had been set up to settle disputes, judge points of law, and decide such questions as the amount of Dane-geld each person must pay. They were attended by representatives of the crown, church officials, sheriffs, land owners, and farmers.

The Anglo-Saxon kings of England had faced the same problems as the early kings of France and Germany. In addition, they followed certain old Anglo-Saxon customs which gave them still more problems. The army and navy, for example, were made up mainly of landholders who were supposed to serve in the armed forces whenever they were called up for duty. It was hard to discipline such men. In fact, William was able to cross the Channel without a battle because the men of the English navy had grown tired of waiting for the invasion and had gone home to gather the harvest. The English kings were also hindered by a group of advisers known as the "witan." While these advisers had little power and their duties were vague, they could make it difficult for the king to reach a decision on any matter.

William the Conqueror promptly introduced into England the feudal system of western Europe. He combined it with the firm central government he had developed in Normandy, and he set out at once to assert his authority over the nobles. Scattered revolts and uprisings throughout England gave him the excuse to claim all the lands of the country as his own. He declared that, by rebelling, the nobles had fofeited their lands and that they now belonged to the king.

mistake again. He was right. He led another charge, pretended to retreat, lured a large number of the English troops into the open, and crushed them. The rest of the English continued to fight. At last, when it was almost night, an arrow pierced King Harold's eye, and he toppled from his horse. The French knights immediately fell upon him and hacked him into pieces. With their leader gone, the English soldiers fled or surrendered on the field. After nine hours of fighting, the battle was over. William had won a crown and a kingdom.

From Hastings, William led his troops up the road to London. News of his great victory went before him, and the people of London decided to submit to the Normans. Many of their nobles and leaders came out to welcome William the Conqueror and surrender the city formally, and on Christmas day of 1066 he was crowned king of England.

THE NOBLES HAD TO GIVE GREAT FEASTS
WHEN WILLIAM CAME TO VISIT THEM.

Having made the entire kingdom into his personal domain, William then began to reward the nobles who had helped him by giving them grants of land. He destroyed strongholds which might be centers of rebellion, and built new castles throughout England, putting them in charge of his most loyal followers. No castle or manor house could be built without William's permission, and no nobleman could get permission to build until he had furnished proof of his loyalty to William and pledged his military support. Each lord was told exactly how many knights he must provide in case of war, and private wars among the nobles were strictly forbidden. The nobles were also forbidden to issue money; only the king had that right.

Although William brought feudalism to England, he made sure that the king had power over the feudal lords. He made just as sure that he would have power over the church. In this he was unlike the other monarchs of Europe, who, when they were not feuding with the church, sought its support against the nobles. From the beginning, William was determined to rule supreme. He appointed bishops and abbots. The English church could not carry out any papal commands without the king's approval.

THE ENGLISH LANGUAGE

One of the unintended results of the conquest was the creation of the English language. For some years after the conquest, nobles and members of the court spoke Norman French, while the rest of the people continued to speak their ancient Anglo-Saxon tongue. Gradually the two languages merged, to become, in time, Middle English and then modern English.

Like Charlemagne two centuries before, William traveled constantly about the land, attending to government matters, sitting in on legal cases, visiting nobles. He traveled with a huge party of nobles, knights, and servants, and if they prolonged their stay at a castle, they could bring their host close to bankruptcy. A steward's records show that once, in a few days of Christmas feasting, William's party devoured 6,000 chickens, 1,000

rabbits, 90 boars, 50 peacocks, 200 geese, and 10,000 eels, as well as thousands of eggs and loaves of bread and hundreds of casks of wine and cider.

THE DOMESDAY BOOK

One of William's greatest achievements came in the last years of his life, when he ordered the compiling of the "Domesday Book." This was a survey of his entire kingdom and all its resources. He sent agents to every shire in England to find out "the name of each manor, who held it in the time of King Edward, who holds it now; the number of hides; the number of plows on the demesne, the number of those of the men; the number of villeins; the number of cotters; the number of serfs; the number of freemen; the number of sokemen; the amount of forest; the amount of meadow; the number of pastures; the number of mills; the number of fishponds; how much it has been increased or diminished; how much it was

all worth then; and how much now; how much each freeman and sokeman held and holds there. All this three times over, namely, in the time of King Edward, and when King William gave it, and as it now is, and if more can be had than is had. . . ." Filling two huge volumes, the Domesday Book was an invaluable social record and became one of England's treasures.

William's reign, which changed the course of English history, ended in 1087. At the age of 64, while in France, in an area north of Paris, making war against Philip I of France, William was stepped on and crushed by his horse. He was succeeded by the eldest of his three sons, William II, who was known as William Rufus and William the Red. William II taxed his people mercilessly, and he was killed in 1100 by an arrow shot by an unknown person.

William's second son was out of the country on a crusade, and Henry I, the youngest of the three sons, took the opportunity to seize the throne. He proved to be a vigorous and efficient ruler. He organized a secretarial department of the government known as the Chancery, and a treasury department known as the Exchequer. The treasury department took its name from the custom of laying out tax payments on a long cloth marked out in squares, or chequers. Each square indicated a certain amount of money, and special markers were placed on them to show how much money had been paid in and how much was still owed. In this way, even a tax collector who could not read could tell how much money he had yet to collect.

CIVIL WAR

After Henry died in 1135, his nephew, Stephen of Blois, became king. But Henry's daughter, Matilda, also claimed the throne, and England was torn by civil war. Without a strong king to hold them in check, the nobles fought and murdered and tortured and plundered. So bad were the nineteen years of Stephen's reign that a chronicler wrote: "I cannot and may not tell of

481

all the wounds, and all the tortures . . . inflicted upon the wretched men of this land. . . . Then was corn dear, and flesh (meat), and cheese, and butter, for there was none in the land—the wretched men starved with hunger—some lived on alms who had been erewhile rich; some fled the country . . . and it was said openly that Christ and His saints slept."

THOMAS À BECKET

Then, in 1154, Henry Plantagenet of Anjou became king. This was the same Henry of Anjou who married Eleanor of Aquitaine after she was divorced from Louis VII of France. Short, stocky, red-haired and freckled, a man of boundless energy and keen intelligence, Henry II was one of the greatest kings of England. He had an uncontrollable temper, and when he was carried away by rage he would roll on the ground, crying, shouting, swearing. He fought many wars on the continent, and he quarreled time after time with his sons and with his wife, whom he finally threw into prison. At the same time, he put down the nobles, restored the power of the monarchy, and brought peace and order to the land. Perhaps even more important, he made many reforms in the law—reforms that led to trial by jury and greater justice for all Englishmen. Henry's many changes in the law established important principles and woud have an influence far beyond his own times; they were the foundation of the legal system of Britain and the United States.

Early in his reign, Henry appointed Thomas à Becket, an educated but not very well known churchman, as his chancellor, an important officer of the realm. Although Becket was more than ten years older than Henry, the two men were soon inseparable—they rode together, drank together, feasted together. Becket became the young and inexperienced king's closest friend and most trusted adviser. And there was much to advise Henry on, for he was interested in everything that went on in his kingdom. He rewrote the tax laws, introduced traveling judges to administer quick and honest judgment and formed a special Court of the King's Bench. He ordered the building of county jails and dikes for flood control He saw to it that beer and bread were sold at fair prices and were of good quality. To strengthen and enlarge his kingdom, Henry made a number of military expeditions to Ireland, Scotland, and France. Becket served as his aide, went on diplomatic missions, and sometimes even fought in the field.

Finally, Henry appointed Becket as archbishop of Canterbury, the head of the Church in England. As part of his campaign to restore the power of the monarchy, Henry was trying to win control over church affairs, and he expected Becket to support and help him. To his shocked surprise, he found that Becket jealously guarded the rights of the church. Now that he was archbishop, Becket felt that he owed loyalty only to the Church. The two men who had once been friends opposed each other on many issues. Their sharpest and most bitter disagreement was over the right of the Church to place clergymen on trial in its own courts instead of the royal courts, to punish them if necessary, and to allow them to make legal appeals to the pope.

MURDER IN THE CATHEDRAL

For six years the struggle between Henry and Becket went on. Once Becket fled to France, returning only after Henry, under pressure from the pope, agreed to make peace with him. But there could be no real peace between them. They continued to oppose each other, until, in a fit of wild

rage, Henry cried out, "What cowards I have about me that no one will deliver me from this lowborn priest!"

Four of Henry's knights believed that he wanted Becket dead. They left the court and set out for Canterbury. Henry was soon sorry for his outburst; it could not have been the first time he said something in anger and regretted it later. But this time he could not stop the violence his words had touched off. The four knights attacked Becket as he celebrated mass at the high altar in Canterbury cathedral and killed him with their swords.

A wave of horror swept over England and spread to the Continent. Henry, too, was horrified. When he learned of the murder in the cathedral, he shut himself off from everyone for three days, neither eating nor drinking. Pope Alexander promptly placed Henry's duchy of Normandy under interdict—a punishment, almost as terrible as excommunication, which forbade the sacraments and Christian burial to all the people of Normandy.

Like the German king, also named Henry, who stood in the snow at Canossa, Henry also made a pilgrimage of penitence. Barefoot and wearing a hairshirt, he walked the streets of Canterbury to the cathedral. There, before the high altar, he bared his back and was flogged by a monk. To complete his penance, he agreed that the Church should have the right to put on trial and punish its clergy, and that the clergy would have the right to appeal to papal courts.

Within two years, in 1173, Thomas à Becket

THE NOBLES FORCED KING JOHN TO SIGN
MAGNA CARTA, OR THE GREAT CHARTER.

was canonized as a saint. The cathedral at Canterbury became a holy place of pilgrimage, and it remained so until it was destroyed during the reign of Henry VIII. Although he was still popular with his people, Henry II's last years were full of strife. His sons, Richard and John, were in constant revolt against him, aided by their mother, Queen Eleanor. In 1189, at the age of 56, Henry died. He had just been defeated in a war, and his last words were: "Shame! Shame on a beaten king!"

RICHARD THE LION-HEARTED

Henry's son Richard then came to the throne. Known as Richard the Lion-Hearted, he was a mighty warrior. He would long be remembered in legends that told of his courage and his great feats on the field of battle. If he had been as good at ruling as he was at fighting, he would have been a great king. But during the ten years of his reign, he spent less than six months in England. His chief interest in his kingdom was to milk it of funds for his wars.

While returning from a crusade to free Jerusalem from Saladin, Richard was taken prisoner by Leopold of Austria. Leopold turned him over to Emperor Henry IV of Germany, who at that time was an ally of Philip Augustus of France. The German emperor refused to free Richard unless he was paid a ransom of 50,000 marks. To raise this enormous sum, new taxes were levied on the people of England, who also had to give up much gold, silver, and other property. As soon as he was free, Richard hurried to England to raise still more money for a new war against France. During the fighting, when he was laying siege to a castle, Richard was struck in the shoulder with an arrow. Gangrene set in, and within a few hours the Lion-Heart was dead.

Richard's successor was his brother, John, who was crowned in 1199. He was cruel, treacherous, and greedy, but during his reign occurred two events which would bring lasting benefit to the English people. The first was the loss of most of the English possessions in France, including Normandy, Maine, Anjou, Touraine, and Brittany. Although it seemed a great calamity at the time, it helped to unify the people of the British Isles. Their fortunes now depended on the English state, and not on the lands across the Channel. They stopped thinking of themselves as Saxons or Normans; instead, they thought of themselves as Englishmen.

The second event was the signing of *Magna Carta,* the Great Charter, which was the foundation of the rights of Englishmen. It came about because of John's failure as a ruler, and particularly because of the crushing burden of the taxes he imposed. As discontent grew everywhere in England, the nobles determined that something must be done to check the king. But defying the king was dangerous, and the nobles moved cautiously, slowly gaining support from the Church and the townspeople. At last, when they were ready to act, a group of lords, church officials, and town leaders presented King John with a petition known as *Magna Carta.* One June 15, 1215, in a meadow outside London, called Runnymede,

the king affixed his seal to the document, agreeing to its demands.

The charter consisted of sixty-three separate chapters; it granted certain rights to the English people and limited the king's power. Most important of all, it contained this statement: "No free man shall be taken or imprisoned or dispossessed, or outlawed or banished, or in any way destroyed . . . except by the legal judgment of his peers or by the law of the land. To no one will we sell, to no one will we deny, or delay right or justice."

MAGNA CARTA

Although it was the upper classes that at first benefited most from *Magna Carta,* it eventually formed the basis of an English constitution. In submitting to the force of his nobles and signing the charter, John was recognizing the right of the English people to make demands of the monarchy and to have a part in making the laws under which they lived. He was also accepting the principle that the king was subject to the law and could not stand above it—a principle that would hold for all the English kings to come.

Nevertheless, *Magna Carta* did not end the trouble between John and his subjects, and his nobles rebelled against him. John rallied his troops to put down the rebellion, but he died in the midst of the campaign, after eating too many fresh peaches and drinking to much new cider. His nine-year-old son, Henry III, now became king. Although his regents managed to put down the revolt, the nobles went on trying to limit royal power and gain greater authority for themselves. Their leader was Simon de Montfort, and in 1265 he succeeded in calling together representatives of all the townships and shires and establishing England's first parliament. A new chapter in English history was beginning.

The Power of the Church
529-1409

IN THE YEAR 1134, in the town of Chartres in France, the church burned down. The church was a cathedral—that is, it was the church of a bishop. The bishop at that time was Theodoric, and he immediately began the construction of another cathedral. He knew that the task would not be an easy one; it meant raising large sums of money and finding many workmen, and the actual work of building would take years.

But Bishop Theodoric allowed nothing to stop him, and he won the support of the people, of commoners and nobles alike. An eye-witness, who visited Chartres in 1144, wrote that "kings, princes, mighty men of the world, puffed up with honors and riches, men and women of noble birth," helped in the work, pulling wagons loaded with "wine, corn, oil, lime, stones, beams, and other things necessary to sustain life or build churches. . . ." And, although a thousand men and women were drawing wagons, "yet they go forward in such silence that no voice, no murmur, is heard. . . . When they pause on the way no words are heard but confessions of guilt, with supplications and pure prayer. . . . The priests preach peace, hatred is soothed, discord is driven away, debts are forgiven, unity is restored."

The cathedral was complete in 1180, but fourteen years later a fire broke out again, destroying most of the building. It also destroyed the townspeople's houses. They would have given up both the church and the town if it had not been for a representative of the pope. The fire was God's punishment for their sins, he warned, and now they must restore the cathedral and put up new houses. The townspeople did as he said. Money for the rebuilding of the church came from the clergy of the area and from cathedrals throughout Europe; hundreds of men and women joined in the work, as they had before; and in 1224 every stone was in place. The great cathedral stood with its spires reaching toward the sky—a masterpiece of Gothic architecture and a monument to the faith of the Middle Ages.

STATUES ON CHARTRES CATHEDRAL.

In the years since the cathedral was first begun, sculptors had worked to adorn it with statues. There were thousands of them—figures of Christ and the Virgin Mary, of the disciples, of prophets, of angels and devils, kings and queens. On the south porch of the cathedral was Christ seated on the judgment seat, surrounded by 783 figures. Besides the sculptors, many other craftsmen had contributed to the beauty and splendor of the cathedral. Workers in stained glass had made the windows that blazed and glowed with color. Workers in iron, brass, gold, and silver had fashioned candlesticks, screens, gates, altar rails, and hinges for the doors. Jewelers had set precious stones in the vessels used for celebrating the mass. Weavers had made velvets and brocades for the altar cloths. Lace makers had made lace to cover the communion table. Wood carvers had carved figures and decorations on the choir stalls, the lecterns, the pulpits, and the screens.

Chartres was only one of the many cathedrals built during the Middle Ages. From 1140 to 1250, building was also begun on the cathedrals of Paris, Bourges, Rheims, and Bayoux. A cathedral was always built on a public square, surrounded by the houses of the townspeople, for it was the religious center of the community.

THE SEVEN SACRAMENTS

If the cathedral was the center of religion, religion was the center of life in the Middle Ages. The word "catholic" means universal, and the Catholic Church was indeed the universal church of western Europe. No man, whether he was serf or peasant, craftsman or merchant, knight or duke or king, could go to heaven unless he followed the beliefs and teachings of the Roman Catholic Church.

The Church taught that because Adam had sinned and was cast out from the Garden of Eden, all mankind was tainted with original sin from birth. To remove this sin, God sent his son, Jesus Christ, to earth, and through Christ's death, man could be saved. Man was helpless to save himself; salvation could come only through God's grace. And grace and salvation could be attained only through the Church itself. Grace was given to men through the practice of certain ceremonies, called sacaments. The seven sacraments were baptism, confirmation, penance, the eucharist, or Lord's supper, extreme unction, and holy

THEY DEPICT BIBLICAL FIGURES.

487

orders. The sacrament of holy orders was administered only to men who entered the clergy.

For those who defied the will of the Church, there were two terrible methods of punishment—excommunication and interdict. Excommunication, as pronounced by Pope Gregory on Emperor Henry IV, deprived a person of the rights of membership in the Church, including the sacraments, and thus condemned his soul to hell. Interdict was the punishment for groups of people, areas, and individual churches. It forbade all public functions of the Church, which included Christian marriage and burial.

THE CLERGY

The Catholic Church of the Middle Ages was truly international. Although its members lived in many different states under many different rulers, the Church had its own lands, its own financial system, its own laws and courts of justice. At the head of the Church was the bishop of Rome, who was called the pope. His authority was based on the words of Jesus, who said to his disciple Simon Peter: "And I say unto thee that thou art Peter, and upon this rock I will build my church, and the gates of hell will not prevail against it. . . ." Since St. Peter had become the first bishop of Rome, this city was accepted as the capital of the Catholic faith, and the bishop of Rome as the leader of the Church. Next in importance to the pope were the cardinals, the "princes" of the Church, who elected as pope one of their own number.

Ranking just below the cardinals were the archbishops. An archbishop was the head of a large ecclesiastical province, just as a duke was the head of a large feudal fief. An archbishop served as bishop to one cathedral in his province, usually the largest and most important. He celebrated mass there on special occasions and certain saints' days. His province was subdivided into areas called dioceses, and he spent a good part of his time in travel, seeing to the affairs of his dioceses and attending various councils in Rome.

Each diocese was headed by a bishop, who was frequently a power in his community. Bishops controlled cathedral lands, monasteries, and other property, and played an important part in the structure of feudalism. Because of their rank, wealth, and training, they were often advisers to nobles or kings, and sometimes provided them

with military aid. Throughout the Middle Ages, popes and kings struggled for the right to appoint bishops.

The day-to-day work of the Church fell to the priests. They were divided into two classes—the secular clergy and the regular clergy. The term "secular" came from the Latin word *saeculum,* which means "world"; the secular clergy lived in the world and ministered to ordinary worshipers. The term "regular" came from the Latin word *regula,* which meant "rule"; the regular clergy were the monks who lived apart from the world in monasteries and governed every moment of their lives by definite rules.

A secular priest was assigned to a parish, a district in which lived all the people who worshiped in his church. In the rural areas, a parish was usually a manorial village. A town might have several parishes, depending on the size of the population. Parish priests almost always came from the common people, but serfs were not permitted to take holy orders.

The parish priest of the Middle Ages had many duties. He was responsible for the regular services of the Church and special services on feast days. He supervised the morals of his parishioners. He conducted services at weddings, baptisms, and funerals, and visited the sick. His income came partly from parish land, partly from fees for marriages, baptisms, and funerals, and partly fom the tithe. The tithe was the contribution made by the parishioners to the Church; each was supposed to give a tenth of his income. A fourth of the tithe went to the parish priest, a fourth for the maintenance of church property, a fourth to the poor, and the remaining fourth to the bishop.

The chief concern of the parish priest was the salvation and welfare of his parishioners; the chief concern of the monk was the salvation of his own soul. Living apart from the world in monasteries, the monks spent long hours in prayer. The rest of their time they spent in meditation, reading religious works, and doing manual labor. At most monasteries, the monks grew the food they ate and made the clothing they wore. Besides the ordinary crops, they often grew medicinal herbs and made such things as wine and cloth.

Monks ate and drank sparingly, and observed a number of fasts. Some monks lived under a vow of silence. Others believed that to endure suffering was a mark of religious devotion; they "mortified the flesh" by wearing a hairshirt next to the skin or a heavy chain fastened around the waist. Sometimes they flogged themselves until the blood flowed and they collapsed with pain.

The practices followed by the monks during the Middle Ages had their beginning in 529. In that year St. Benedict founded the parent monastery of the Benedictine order of monks at Monte Cassino in Italy. There had been monks before, but they lived according to no real plan, and many went to extremes of fasting and mortifying the flesh. In his community of monks, St. Benedict established a daily routine of worship and manual labor. For the next few centuries, because of their hard work and devotion to religion, the Benedictines flourished.

As the power of the monks increased, however, they became less disciplined, and in 910 a reform movement began at the monastery in Cluny. The Cluniacs insisted that their abbots, the heads of their monasteries, be elected by the monks themselves, rather than appointed by kings or nobles. They also called for a reform of the secular clergy. All priests and church officials, they said, should be appointed by the Church and not by feudal lords. The popes welcomed the Cluniac reforms as a way to rid the Church of any control by the lords.

In the twelfth century, St. Bernard of Clairvaux believed it was time for new reforms. A French nobleman, he took holy orders in 1112 and became the most famous churchman of his

THIS MEDIEVAL MANUSCRIPT SHOWS THE ROBES OF DIFFERENT ORDERS OF MONKS.

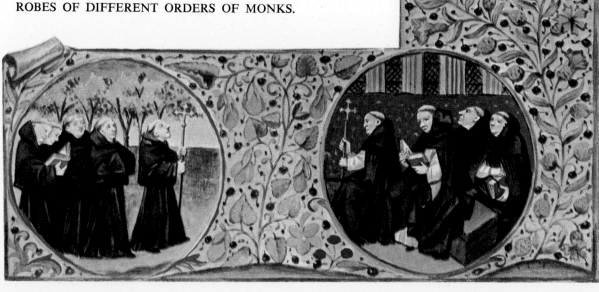

THE CHURCH IN THE MIDDLE AGES HANGED OR BURNED MANY HERETICS. IN THE FORE-GROUND, ST. FRANCIS AND ST. DOMINIC.

age. He founded the Cistercian order of monks, preached the second crusade, and never stopped urging the clergy to keep their vows.

It was the practice of the nobles and kings to give the monasteries vast tracts of land, usually wild and wooded. By hard labor, the monks cleared the land and brought it under cultivation. In this way, many monasteries acquired great and rich estates that rivalled those of even the wealthiest of feudal lords.

THE FRIARS

By the thirteenth century, monks of a new kind had appeared. The called themselves "friars," from *frater,* the Latin word for brother. They wanted to bring religion directly to the people, and instead of shutting themselves off from the world they went to live in the cities. Without monasteries to support them, they depended on the charity of the people. For this reason the

orders of friars were called mendicant, or begging, orders.

SAINT FRANCIS

Two of the mendicant orders became widely known. One was the Franciscans, which was founded by the gentle St. Francis of Assisi. The son of a successful merchant, Francis was born in 1182 in the little hill town of Assisi in Italy. His father tried to make a soldier of him, but Francis was a cheerful, amiable young man who was more interested in music, poetry, and the company of his friends than he was in war. He was captured during a battle, imprisoned for several years, and then became ill with a fever. When he had recovered from his illness, he decided to change his life. He would dedicate himself to God, helping the poor and the sick. Wishing to be like Jesus Christ, he gave up all his property and possessions and dressed in a beggar's rags. Gentle and hum-

490

ble, he loved all living things, and it was said that he preached to the birds. The followers who gathered about him in great numbers were recognized by the pope as the Franciscans.

The other mendicant order that became widely known was the Dominicans. It was founded by St. Dominic, a Spanish-born monk, and it grew out of his experience in fighting heresy in southern France. Heresy was the belief in doctrines that differed from the accepted doctrines of the Catholic Church. The Church allowed certain criticisms, but beliefs that went too far and seemed dangerous to the Church were condemned as heresy. St. Dominic insisted that the Church needed learned and well-educated preachers and teachers to explain its beliefs to the people and prevent them from becoming heretics.

THE INQUISITION

And heresy was a problem to the Church in the Middle Ages, particularly during the thirteenth century. Its very existence was threatened by two great heresies—those of the Waldensians and the Albigensians.

The Waldensians took their name from Peter Waldo, a merchant of Lyons in France. Waldo gave his riches to the poor and founded a lay order of monks—that is, monks who were not ordained as priests. They traveled about, preaching to the people, and their beliefs spread to a number of countries. They based their ideas directly on the New Testament of the Bible. They criticised the morals of the clergy, and some Waldensians went even further. They said that there was no need for the clergy or the mass or the sacraments; all that a good Christian needed was the Bible. It was a challenge to the authority of the Church, and in 1118 they were condemned as heretics. Driven underground by persecution, they continued to spread their beliefs, which in years to come would influence the Protestants of France and Hussites of Bohemia. The Waldensians could well be called the first Protestants of Europe.

Unlike the Waldensians, the Albigensians, who were most active in southern France, kept little of the orthodox Christian faith. They believed that Satan, an Evil God, was in conflict with the Good God. Some day the Good God would be victorious, but until that day the world was ruled by Satan—and the Catholic clergy were in league with him. Albigensians who sought perfection could not marry, and could not eat meat, cheese, milk, or eggs; they refused to swear oaths of any kind and were opposed to taking part in any war. They were a danger to the state as well as to the Church, and the king of France joined the pope in a crusade to wipe them out completely.

But heresy could never be wiped out completely, and there was no telling when it would rise again. The Church was determined to put down heresy, and in 1229 the Council of Toulouse established the Ecclesiastical Inquisition. Four years later Pope Gregory IX set up the Court of Inquisition. The inquisitors would give the people of an area a month to come forward and confess heresy. Those who did confess were given a light punishment. When the month was over, persons suspected of heresy were brought to trial. The accusation of two witnesses was enough to bring anyone before the inquisitors, and there was little the accused person could do to defend himself. The object of the trial was to win a confession from the accused person, so that he could be punished and brought back into the Church. Those who refused to confess were often tortured, and a small number were turned over to the state to be burned at the stake.

THE UNIVERSITIES

It was the battle against heresy that helped give rise to the institution of learning known as the university. Before, there had been schools connected with monasteries and cathedrals. But in the twelfth and thirteenth centuries, when various heresies were springing up, the Church needed to train men to defend the beliefs of Catholicism. There were additional reasons, just as important, for the rise of the universities. One was the interest of the Dominican friars in education. Another was the learning that was reaching Europe from the Arabic countries, particularly Islamic Spain. Many books were translated from Arabic into Latin, or were first translated into Hebrew by Jewish scholars living in Spain, and then into Latin. Still another reason was that, with the increase in population and the growth of towns, both the Church and the nobility needed men trained in the law and still more men to handle the work of administration.

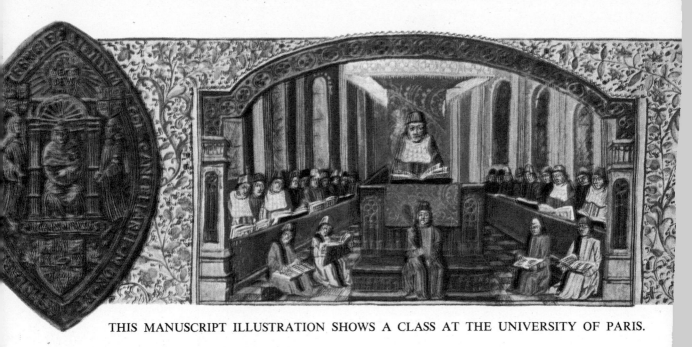

THIS MANUSCRIPT ILLUSTRATION SHOWS A CLASS AT THE UNIVERSITY OF PARIS.

In their early days, the universities of the Middle Ages were run by the students themselves, who chose their subjects, their professors, and even their hours of study. At first the universities had no buildings of their own, and classes met in any place that was available. Books were scarce and expensive, and the students had none, but the master, or professor, lectured from his own books and manuscripts. The students tried to memorize as much of the lecture as they could; many took notes on parchment or on wax tablets, which were cheaper. Later they would meet in taverns to compare notes and discuss the lecture.

The principal subject was theology, the study of religion. The theories of such great churchmen as Thomas Aquinas were taught, as well as the theories of Aristotle, the Greek thinker. Other subjects were arithmetic, astronomy, Latin, gram-

A MEDIEVAL STONE CARVING OF STUDENTS AT THE UNIVERSITY OF BOLOGNA

mar, music, law, and medicine. As the universities began to win financial support from noblemen and rich merchants, they grew in size and importance. Some specialized in certain branches of learning. The University of Paris was famous for theological studies, the University of Bologna, in Italy, for law, the University of Salamanca, in Spain, for medicine. Other noted universities founded during this period were those at Oxford, Cambridge, Prague, Leipzig, and Heidelberg.

THE POWER OF THE POPE

But the influence of the Church went far beyond the universities; it was largely the Church that kept learning alive in the Middle Ages. The monks copied and illuminated manuscripts, and the bishops built great cathedrals. Painting, sculpture, music—all showed the influence of the Church. Townspeople performed in mystery and miracle plays, based on tales from the Bible; these were the forerunner of modern drama. Latin, the official language of the Church, was the international language of all educated men during the Middle Ages.

Most of Europe was unified in faith and culture, and this gave the Church, and its head, the pope, vast political power. Many churchmen dreamed of a universal state under the pope, and this led to conflicts between the Church and the rulers of Europe. The popes of the Middle Ages played an important part in shaping political events; they stopped and started wars, launched crusades, and made and unmade kings. No pope of this period wielded as much power and influence as Pope Innocent III, who reigned from 1198 to 1216. The popes who followed steadily lost power as they supported the kings of France against the English kings and the Holy Roman emperors. Finally Clement VII, a pope who had been born in France, had to flee Rome and take refuge in Avignon, in the south of France, where he could be protected by the French king.

The people and the government of Rome demanded an Italian pope. Supported by the Holy Roman emperor, they elected a second pope. For more than forty years there were two popes, and at one time there were even three men who each claimed to be the true pope. The Great Schism,

THE CATHEDRAL OF AMIENS IN FRANCE IS A MASTERPIECE OF GOTHIC ARCHITECTURE.

as this split in the Church was called, lessened the authority of the Roman Catholic Church throughout Europe.

In 1409, a general council of Church leaders and scholars was called in Pisa, Italy, to take over the direction of the Church and decide on the true pope. This was part of the Conciliar Movement, whose aim was to make the pope subject to a council of bishops and archbishops. The movement failed in its attempts to reorganize and reform the Church, and the papacy never regained the power it had held. But for centuries during the Middle Ages the Roman Catholic Church had an enormous influence on the thought and actions of men, an influence that left its mark on Western civilization.

THE CRUSADERS BUILT STRONG FORTRESSES IN THE HOLY LAND.

The Crusades
1096-1260

ON A COLD NOVEMBER DAY IN 1096, a great crowd of people gathered in a field at the town of Clermont in France. They had come from miles around, and near them were pitched the tents they had put up for shelter. For some days, Pope Urban II had been holding a great council of cardinals, bishops, and princes. Today he was to speak to the people, and so many wanted to hear that no building was large enough to hold them all. A platform had been built in the center of the field, and as Pope Urban stepped up on it a hush fell over the crowd.

Pope Urban was a Frenchman, and he spoke to the people around him as fellow Frenchmen. "Oh, race of Franks," he said, "race beloved and chosen by God . . . set apart from all other nations by the situation of your country as well as by your Catholic faith and the honor which you render to the holy Church: to you our discourse is addressed. . . .

"From the confines of Jerusalem and from Constantinople a grievous report has gone forth that an accursed race, wholly alienated from God, has violently invaded the lands of these Chris-

tians, and has depopulated them by pillage and fire. They have led away a part of the captives into their own country, and a part they have killed by cruel tortures. . . ."

The people knew what he meant. He was speaking of the Holy Land, that lay on the eastern shores of the Mediterranean Sea. Here were the cities of Jerusalem, Nazareth, Gaza, and Damascus. Here Jesus Christ had lived and preached and had been crucified; here Christianity had begun. Here were many sacred shrines, and during the Middle Ages thousands of Europeans had made pilgrimages to see them.

"IT IS THE WILL OF GOD!"

The Holy Land had been part of the Byzantine Empire, after the fall of the Roman Empire. Then, in 638, Arab troops led by the Caliph Omar had defeated a Byzantine army and had gone on to conquer all of Asia Minor, including the Holy Land. The Arabs, or Saracens, as they were called in Europe, were Moslems. But they did not interfere with the Christians living in the Holy Land, nor did they interfere with the bands of pilgrims who came from western Europe during the next four centuries to visit the sacred places. In 1070, however, Jerusalem fell into the hands of the Turks. They, too, were Moslems, and stories of the persecution of Christians began to reach Europe.

The people who stood on the field at Clermont

had heard such stories, and they listened closely as Pope Urban went on with his speech.

"On whom, then," he said, "rests the labor of avenging these wrongs, and of recovering this territory, if not upon you—you upon whom, above all others, God has conferred remarkable glory in arms, great bravery, and strength to humble the heads of those who resist you? . . . Let none of your possessions keep you back, nor anxiety for your family affairs. For this land which you now inhabit, shut in on all sides by the sea and the mountain peaks, is too narrow for your large population; it scarcely furnishes food enough for its cultivators. Here it is that you murder and devour one another, that you wage wars, and that many among you perish in civil strife.

"Let hatred, therefore, depart from among you; let your quarrels end. Enter upon the road to the Holy Sepulcher; wrest that land from a wicked race, and subject it to yourselves. . . . This royal city . . . is now held captive by the enemies of Christ and is subjected by those who do not know God, to the worship of the heathen. . . . Undertake this journey eagerly for the remission of your sins, with the assurance of the reward of imperishable glory in the kingdom of heaven."

A murmur ran through the crowd. The pope was calling for war—a holy war against the Turks, against the Moslems, to win back Jerusalem and put it once more under Christian rule. And what true Christian would not fight such a war, for the glory of God?

"It is the will of God!" the people shouted. "It is the will of God! It is the will of God!"

Lifting his eyes to heaven, Pope Urban raised a hand for silence and gave thanks to God. Let that be their war cry: "It is the will of God!" And let everyone who joined in this holy war wear the sign of the cross of the Lord on his forehead or on his breast. And he ended his speech—perhaps the most important speech made during the Middle Ages—by saying: "Thus shall ye . . . fulfill the precept of the Lord, as he commands in the Gospel, 'He that taketh not his cross, and followeth after me, is not worthy of me.' "

Again the shout went up: "It is the will of God! It is the will of God!" At the same time,

THIS 12TH CENTURY STATUE SHOWS A CRUSADER WELCOMED HOME BY HIS WIFE.

some of the nobles in the crowd, as a chronicler later wrote, "falling down at the knees of the pope, consecrated themselves and their property to the service of God."

After he had roused up the people, Pope Urban did not linger long in Clermont. For nine months he traveled from city to city preaching the holy war, the Crusade. A former Cluniac monk, he deeply believed it was the responsibility of the Church to free the Holy Land from Moslem rule and spread the doctrine of Catholicism. But he had other reasons as well to want this war. For one thing, the Byzantine Emperor, Alexius Comnenus of Constantinople, had asked for help in his long struggle to recapture lands that had been taken from him by the Moslems. Pope Urban saw that this was an opportunity to re-unite the Greek Church and the Roman Catholic Church and place all of Christendom under the authority of the pope. And then Urban was involved in a struggle of his own, a struggle for power against the monarchs of Europe. He would have a better chance of winning that struggle if the kings and nobles were off on a crusade.

Wherever he went, Pope Urban found enthusiasm for the crusade. People were growing more and more angry at the thought that the land of Christ's birth was under the rule of infidels; like Urban, they believed it was their duty as Christians to win back the Holy Land. But, also like Urban, many had other reasons, too, for supporting this holy war. The nobles hoped to win new lands and territories for themselves in the East. Knights-at-arms hoped for plunder and loot. Serfs and peasants hoped to escape from the land to which they were bound, and to leave behind a life of harsh restrictions and terrible poverty.

THE FIRST CRUSADE

And so nobles and knights, serfs and freemen flocked to the crusader's standard—a red cross on a white banner. Knights had the same design put on their shields, and foot soldiers sewed a red cross to their white tunics.

In all, there were eight different crusades, extending over a period of several hundred years.

CRUSADERS WORE HEAVY HELMETS AND SUITS OF CHAIN MAIL FOR PROTECTION.

The first army of crusaders, made up almost entirely of serfs and peasants, was to leave in August of 1096. Excited by the promise of adventure and the hope of breaking out of their miserable existence, they could not wait. In March about 12,000 persons, led by Peter the Hermit and Walter the Penniless, left from France, while two other groups set out from Germany and the Rhineland. As they marched through the valleys of the Rhine and Danube, they looted farms and homes and attacked Jews.

At last, ragged and penniless, they reached Constantinople. They swarmed through the city, looting and pillaging, and the Emperor Alexius Comnenus was horrified. He had expected Europe to send him disciplined fighting men, not this mob of unruly peasants. As quickly as he could, he furnished them with ships and supplies and sent them across the Bosporus to Asia Minor. He told them to wait for better equipped reinforcements, but again they were impatient. They marched against the Turkish capital of Nicaea, where they were almost completed wiped out by a force of Turkish bowmen.

The following year, four main armies of Crusaders arrived in Constantinople, most of them knights. Many had brought their wives and children, as well as squires, clerks, cooks, armorers, and blacksmiths. The Byzantine emperor and his courtiers were shocked at their crude manners; the knights, in turn, looked down on the Byzantines, with their elegance and luxury. Some of the knights wanted to seize Constantinople and its riches for themselves. The frightened and suspicious emperor demanded that the nobles swear an oath of allegiance to him. They agreed, after he furnished them with supplies and military aid and bribed their leaders.

The Crusaders' force numbered about 30,000 persons when it advanced into Asia Minor. Fortunately for them, the Turks were having trouble with their own rebels, and Nicaea surrendered after a siege. The Crusaders then pushed on through the fierce heat of Syria. They lacked sufficient food and water, and many died of thirst. But they met little resistance from the Turks until they reached the trading center of Antioch, which fell only after a siege of seven months.

No more than 12,000 Cusaders, led by Raymond of Toulouse, reached Jerusalem in 1099. On July 15 they captured the city from its Egyptian garrison, falling on the defenders without mercy. An eyewitness wrote that "one of our knights, named Lethold, clambered up the wall of the city. . . . Our men followed, killing and slaying even to the Temple of Solomon, where the slaughter was so great that our men waded in blood up to their ankles. . . . When the pagans had been overcome, our men seized great numbers, either killing them or keeping them captive, as they wished. . . . Afterward the army scattered throughout the city and took possession of the gold and silver, the horses and mules, and the houses filled with goods of all kinds. Later all our people went to the Sepulchre of the Lord, rejoicing and weeping for joy. . . ." Another eyewitness wrote that "the amount of blood that they shed on that day is incredible. . . . Piles of heads, hands and feet were to be seen in the streets of the city. . . . The city was filled with corpses and blood."

THE CRUSADE OF KINGS

The capture of Jerusalem was the Crusaders' greatest success in Syria and Palestine, a success they would never be able to repeat. They organized the territory they won into four units—the counties of Edessa and Tripoli, the principality of Antioch, and the Kingdom of Jerusalem. They established feudal courts throughout Syria and Palestine, and certain coastal towns were put under the control of the Italian city-states of Genoa, Pisa, and Venice, in return for their military aid.

During this period, two military orders were formed. They were the Knights Templars and the Knights Hospitallers. The members of these orders combined chivalry with monasticism, taking monastic vows, though not necessarily for life. The Knights Templars dedicated themselves to a life of fighting, but they became known as the bankers and traders of the Crusades. The Knights Hospitallers cared for the sick and the wounded, and assisted pilgrims.

In 1144, a force of Seljuk Turks captured the County of Edessa and destroyed the city of Edessa. This brought about a new Crusade, led by King Louis VII of France, and it was a complete failure. A German army was destroyed in Asia Minor, and the French army receive no cooperation from the Christian leaders they had come to

rescue. The Flemish and English armies never
reached the Holy Land at all. Instead, they went
to Portugal, where they set up a Christian kingdom with Lisbon as the capital.

Then, in 1174, a remarkable man named Saladin became the ruler of Egypt. A brilliant military leader, he set about uniting the Moslem
world. After Moslems from Cairo to Baghdad
had rallied around him, he planned a *jehad,* or
holy war, against the Christians in the East. He
wiped out an army of the Crusaders near Nazareth, swept down through Palestine, and in 1187
took Jerusalem. This time there was no slaughter
of the conquered by the conquerors, for Saladin
was generous to his defeated enemies, and he
won the admiration of many of the Crusaders.

But the fall of Jerusalem aroused western
Europe and set off the Third Crusade. This Crusade has been called "the Crusade of kings." Its
vast armies were led by Emperor Frederick Barbarossa of Germany and the Holy Roman Empire,
King Philip Augustus of France, and Richard the
Lion-Hearted of England—the monarchs of the
three most powerful states in Europe.

Nevertheless, the Third Crusade was as dismal
a failure as the one before it. Frederick Bar-

barossa marched his well-equipped army over the land route, through Hungary and the Balkans. In Asia Minor he drowned while bathing in a river, and many of his troops turned back without striking a blow. Richard and Philip Augustus, who were life-long enemies, quarreled constantly. A courtier noted that "the two kings did less together than they would have done apart, and each set very light store by the other." Somehow they managed to take the cities of Acre, Joppa and, Ascalon—and then Philip Augustus found an excuse to go home.

Although Richard's bravery on the battlefield made him the hero of many legends, he was no match for Saladin. He won many battles, but he could not take Jerusalem. After three years he finally gave up and arranged a truce with Saladin. As his weary men moved away from the city they could not capture, a young knight rode up to Richard, pointed toward a rocky hill, and said, "If you will ride up there, my lord, you will be able to see Jerusalem in the distance." Richard answered, "Those who are not worthy to win the Holy City are not worthy to behold it!" It was while on the way home after this failure that Richard was shipwrecked, captured by Henry VI

SALADIN, RULER OF EGYPT AND A GREAT MILITARY LEADER, CAPTURED JERUSALEM AND DEFEATED THE CRUSADERS.

499

THE MEN OF THE FOURTH CRUSADE, URGED ON BY VENETIAN MERCHANTS,
CAPTURED AND LOOTED THE ANCIENT CHRISTIAN CITY OF CONSTANTINOPLE.

of Germany, and held for ransom. Saladin died in 1193, before he could succeed in driving all the Christians out of the Moslem domain, but he did keep them out of Jerusalem.

Ten years later, the powerful Pope Innocent III called for a fourth crusade. This time the armies were led mainly by French nobles and knights, although they had troops from a number of countries, including England, Germany, Sicily, and Flanders. To avoid the land route, they arranged to set sail from Venice. That city was also to furnish them with ships and supplies. The shrewd Venetians drove a hard bargain. The Crusaders were to pay them the sum of 85,000 marks. Besides, as the Doge of Venice—the head of the Venetian government—put it, "For the love of God we will add to the fleet fifty armed galleys, on condition that, so long as we act in company, of all conquests in land or money, whether at sea or on dry ground, we shall have the half and you the other half."

And so the Crusaders were partners with the city-state of Venice but, as they would learn, it was Venice that would get the profit. When they were ready to set sail, they still owed 34,000 marks; to wipe out the debt, the Venetians insisted that they conquer the Hungarian island of Zara. Against the wishes of the pope—for Zara was a Christian city—the Crusaders took Zara for the Venetians. Then, when they reached Constantinople, they became involved with the complicated politics of the Byzantine Empire. Urged on by the Venetians, they took Constantinople.

For three days, beginning on April 13, 1204, the Crusaders and the Venetians sacked the city, burning, plundering, robbing, slaughtering, in one of the worst riots of destruction in history. Nothing escaped looting—palaces, churches, libraries, homes, shops. A knight who was one of the Crusaders wrote: "The booty gained was so great that none could tell you of it. Gold and silver and vessels and precious stones and samite and cloth of silk and robes, vair and grey, and ermine and every choicest thing found upon the earth. . . . never, since the world was created, had so much booty been won in any city. . . . These defenders of Christ, who should have turned their swords only against infidels, have bathed in Christian blood. They have respected neither religion nor age nor sex. . . . Greatly did they rejoice and give thanks because of the victory God

had vouchsafed to them—for those who before had been poor were now in wealth and luxury."

What the nobles and soldiers could not steal, they destroyed, and many precious manuscripts and works of art were lost. The Venetians, who were well acquainted with Constantinople and its treasures, made off with sculpture, paintings, jewelry and slaves. Among their prizes were the four bronze horses that would stand on Venice's Basilica of San Marco for centuries to come. Nor was that all the Venetians gained. They divided the Byzantine Empire with the Crusaders and Venice became the greatest trade center in Europe.

The results of the Fourth Crusade shocked many people in Europe, but crusading went on. The most tragic of all the crusades, the Children's Crusade, took place in 1212, when thousands of children from France and Germany marched southward to the Mediterranean Sea. They believed it would part for them, as the Red Sea had parted for Moses and the tribes of Israel, and that they could then cross to the Holy Land. Most of the children were stopped and sent home before they reached Genoa, but many of those who went on were sold into slavery.

The Fifth Crusade, in 1218, was another of the failures. The Sixth Crusade was led by Frederick II of Germany. Curiously, by the time he set off in 1228, he had been excommunicated by Pope Gregory IX, with whom he had political differences. Frederick was not too disturbed; he was interested in power rather than religion. A man of learning and sharp intelligence, he relied on negotiations instead of force. He signed a treaty with the Sultan of Egypt, who had his own troubles and preferred to avoid a war with the Christians. The treaty called for a truce of ten years and allowed Frederick the right to be crowned as the king of Jerusalem.

In 1244, St. Louis of France led the Seventh Crusade, in which he was captured by the Turks and forced to pay a heavy ransom. Sixteen years later, while on still another crusade, he died at Carthage. By the end of the thirteenth century, all the territory in the Holy Land which the Crusaders had fought to conquer was again in Moslem hands.

While the Crusaders failed in the end to accomplish what they had set out to do, the Crusades had some important effects on western Europe. They helped to break the power of feudalism; when the feudal lords were away

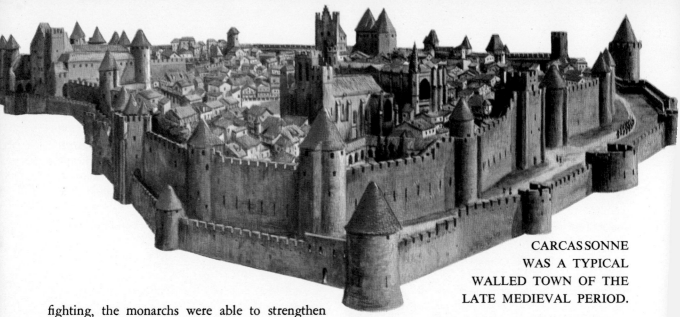

fighting, the monarchs were able to strengthen their authority. The Crusades introduced the West to the highly developed culture of the Byzantines and Moslems, and the luxuries of the East. It opened up new trade routes, and Europe began to import spices, sugar, camphor, musk, lemons, melons, ivory, rugs, tapestries, brocades, and cotton and damask materials.

Europe was no longer cut off from the rest of the world; through the Crusades it had discovered the East.

The Town and the Guild
1100-1382

ONE FINE SPRING MORNING, in the French town of Troyes, in the county of Champagne, a bell rang out through the clear air. The people streaming along the road to the town knew why the bell was ringing; it signaled the start of another day of the fair. Now they walked faster or whipped up their horses, anxious not to miss any of the excitement. Most of them were merchants, who had come to buy the goods that were on display. Some were lords and ladies, who hoped to find gleaming silks from the Orient, or

fine Spanish leather, or rich furs from Russia. The rest were peasants and workmen; they had little money to spend, but they might buy a few small things and they would enjoy the clowns, minstrels, and jugglers who performed for the crowds on the streets.

The fairs of Champagne, held at several towns in that county, had their beginning early in the twelfth century and continued for more than two hundred years. The feudal lords of Champagne, who were called counts, realized that the fairs brought many benefits to them and their people, and wisely did everything they could to make Champagne a center of trade. They built spacious warehouses and pavilions for the storage and display of merchandise. To make it easier for merchants from various parts of the world to do business, the counts set up booths where the money of one territory could be exchanged for the money of another. They established a special court to settle disputes over business dealings, and their troops protected travelers from the bandits who roamed the roads. The counts themselves profited from all this, for they collected fees from the merchants and traders who took part in the fair.

Champagne's location made it easy to reach from any direction. Italian and Swiss merchants could come over the Alps through the St. Bernard pass. Traders from the south could come up the Rhône River. From the west, Champagne could be reached by way of two more rivers, the Loire and the Seine, and from the north by three—the Meuse, the Moselle, and the Rhine.

And so the fairs at Champagne, held throughout the year, became the most important in Europe. Silks, woolens, linen, leather, wine, furs, articles of iron, spices—all were sold at Champagne. But there were fairs in other towns as well. Paris had a fair that was famous throughout Europe. In England, fairs were held at St. Giles, St. Ives, Bartholomew, and Stourbridge; in Flanders, at Ypres, Lille, Thourout, and Bruges.

The success of the fairs was part of the rise in trade that took place in the later centuries of the Middle Ages—and the rise in trade led to the growth of towns. In the early days of feudalism, after the collapse of the Roman Empire, there had been little growth of towns. The decaying roads made travel difficult, and the communities were isolated, cut off from one another. Everything they needed, they produced for themselves —food, clothing, weapons, and household goods.

Slowly, over the years, this isolation was broken down. Italian cities on the Adriatic and Mediterranean seas, such as Venice, Genoa, and Pisa, began trading with the Byzantine Empire. To

GOODS FROM EUROPE AND THE EAST WERE SOLD AT THE MEDIEVAL FAIRS.

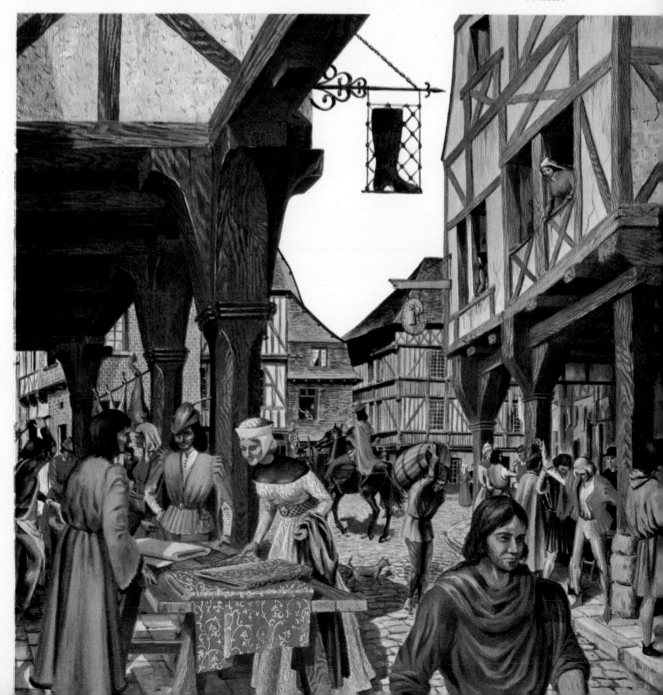

their busy ports ships brought the products of the East, including spices, medicines, and luxury goods such as perfumes, pearls, ivory, and silks. The Crusades also helped to open up new channels of trade between the East and the West.

A NEW CLASS OF MEN

A new class of men came into being, men who were not lords nor knights nor clergymen nor craftsmen. They were the merchants who made long and difficult journeys to seaports, bought the goods brought in by ship, and transported the goods for sale to the cities and towns of Europe. To avoid the bad roads and the robbers that infested them, they began to travel by water, over the many rivers of the continent. By boat and barge they went throughout Italy, Spain, France, Germany, and England. Some merchants, finding a community they particularly liked, and needing the protection of a powerful lord, decided to settle down and open shops.

As trade increased and more shops were opened, the towns grew. Other things, too, helped the towns grow. A new monastery or cathedral might be built, and it would attract scholars and pilgrims, as well as church officials. And serfs from nearby villages, seeking freedom, fled to the towns. Among them were craftsmen, who found that they could earn a living by making clothing or pottery or furniture and selling it to their neighbors.

In time, the feudal rulers came to welcome the growth of towns in their domains. They found that they could add to their wealth by placing taxes on commercial enterprises. They also found that the goods on sale in the towns added to the comfort of their lives.

During the twelfth, thirteenth, and fourteenth centuries, monarchs and noblemen began issuing charters for towns, in return for a sum of money plus a yearly rental fee. Kings were especially eager to grant town charters, both to bring in money and to insure themselves of the town's loyalty. In most of the charters, the lords agreed to consider the town's land as free land. This meant that all residents of the town became

TRADE AND CRAFTS FLOURISHED IN THE TOWNS OF THE MIDDLE AGES.

freemen after living there for a year and a day. "Town air is free air," people said, and to breathe the free air of the towns, many serfs ran away from the manorial villages where they were held in bondage. To protect their independence, some towns banded together, and in this way were formed the Lombard League in northern Italy and the Hanseatic League in Germany.

LIFE IN THE TOWNS

Although the merchants who attended the fairs came from many different places, the towns they returned to were much alike in their general plan. Around every town was a high wall and a moat, with drawbridges at the gates. Near the main gate stood the gallows, and often, as a warning to criminals, the body of a condemned man was left dangling there, or his head was cut off and stuck on one of the spikes over the gate.

Within the wall, except for one street that ran around the entire town, the streets were narrow and crooked. The houses were usually two or three stories tall, although some were as high as seven stories, with overhanging upper stories that cast deep shadows over the unpaved streets. All day long the towns were filled with noise and bustle. Merchants and craftsmen were busy in the open shops. They had little time to glance at the people passing by—peasants carrying live chickens or a basket of eggs, monks in their brown or black habits, students in their billowing gowns, beggars in rags, dawdling schoolboys, and housewives doing their shopping. They had to press back against the walls to make way for carts or horsemen, or noble ladies in litters carried by four attendants. Dogs and pigs were everywhere, feeding on the garbage that was tossed out of the windows, often without warning.

At the center of each town was the paved public square, where markets were held and the people gathered for festivals and processions. On one side of the square stood the cathedral or the town's largest church; on the other sides were the town hall and the halls of the guilds, the associations of merchants and craftsmen.

Townspeople rose early and went to bed early. If they had to go out after dark, they carried lanterns or torches, for there were no street lights. But mostly they stayed indoors; night was the time when robbers lurked in the shadows, and watchmen and guards were few.

Day or night, there was always the danger of fire and disease. The houses were jammed closely together, and fire spread quickly from one to another. In some towns, watchmen carried long hooked poles to pull down burning houses that threatened their neighbors.

Disease spread as quickly as fire, and epidemics, called plagues, were common. Worst of all was the Black Death, an outbreak of bubonic plague

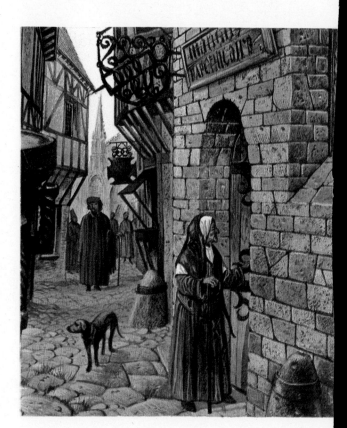

that spread throughout Europe in 1348-49, striking down millions of people. Those who could fled from the towns and cities, where carts rumbled through the streets, piled high with the bodies of the dead.

THE GUILDS

In spite of fire and disease, the towns grew—and the guilds grew with them. The guilds were first started by merchants, to protect themselves against outside competition. They had strict control of all trade within a town, and they regulated prices, the quality of goods, weights, measures, and the methods of doing business. The guilds were so strong that a merchant feared expulsion only less than death itself; to be expelled meant being deprived of a livelihood.

The guilds were religious, social, and welfare organizations as well as business associations. Each guild had its patron saint, and the members

celebrated religious festivals together and often were responsible for putting on religious plays. The guilds looked after their sick and their poor; the rules of one guild stated that when a member became ill, "wine shall be sent to him, two loaves of bread and a gallon of wine, and a dish from the kitchen; and two approved men of the guild shall go to visit him, and look after his condition."

Craftsmen followed the example of merchants and formed guilds of their own. They set stand-

A MEDIEVAL PHARMACY. BELOW, AN ALCHEMIST AT WORK.

ards of workmanship, and members found guilty of faulty work were heavily fined. Working conditions were also carefully regulated, as shown by the rules of the spur-makers, or spurriers, of London: "No one of the trade of spurriers shall work longer than from the beginning of the day until curfew ring out at the Church of St. Sepulchre outside Newgate, by reason that no man can work so neatly by nights as by day . . . nor shall they introduce false iron, and iron that has been cracked, nor put gilt on false copper. . . ."

Craftsmen were divided into three classes—apprentices, journeymen, and masters. To enter a trade, a boy had to work as an apprentice to a master for a term of two to seven years. His parents paid the master a fee; in return, the master furnished the apprentice with food, lodging, and clothes, and taught him the trade. After his term of apprenticeship, the craftsman became a journeyman. This name came from the French word *journée,* which means day; a journeyman had the right to work by the day for wages. To become a master and open his own workshop, a journeyman had to pass an examination and take an oath to abide by the rules of the guild. Often, to show his skill, he also had to submit an example of his work, called a "master's piece."

Members of merchants' guilds were usually the richest men in a town and controlled the town's government. As the merchants became more and more powerful, trouble broke out between their guilds and those of the craftsmen, who wanted their share of the power. Between 1378 and 1382 there were bloody uprisings in Florence, Ghent, and Paris, and in France the king took steps to give the craftsmen more privileges.

But already the merchants were widening their activities, and becoming bankers and industrialists. Europe was moving toward that system of society called capitalism, a system in which the guilds would disappear and craftsmen would be employees working for wages. Altogether, the growth of towns and the guilds led to the breakdown of feudalism and manorialism. Serfs found freedom by running away to the towns, and a man no longer had to be born an aristocrat to have wealth and power. He could gain a fortune for himself in commerce and industry. And the merchants, who needed the law and order that only a central authority could provide, supported the kings against the feudal nobles. The rigid world of the Middle Ages was beginning to change.

The Hundred Years War

1326-1477

THE LONG STRUGGLE between France and England, known to history as the Hundred Years' War, was not really a war—and it lasted more than a hundred years. Rather than a war, it was a series of separate battles, with periods of uneasy

peace between, and it lasted from 1338 to 1453. It was time of misery for both sides, but the French lost more men and saw much of their land devastated. By the end of the Hundred Years' War, important changes had taken place in both countries. In France, the years of conflict weakened the power of the nobility and led to the rise of a strong middle class. And warfare would never be the same; the English victories showed that mounted knights, weighed down by heavy armor, were no match for archers with longbows, and the final battles were decided by artillery.

The cause of the war was that England still held the Duchy of Aquitaine, a rich land in southwestern France, and was determined not to lose it. The French were equally determined to drive them out. A further complication was the situation in Flanders. The English sold raw wool to Flemish manufacturers, who wove it into cloth and sold a good part of it back to the English. This trade was important to England, and even more so to Flanders, and both countries were anxious that nothing should happen to disturb it. The English also kept a watchful eye on the Flemish ports, which could serve as a base for a French attack on England or an English attack on the continent. But Flanders was not a completely independent state; its ruler, the Count of Flanders, owed allegiance to the king of France. England tried to destroy the count's authority by stirring up the Flemish against him. Meanwhile, France aided England's enemies in Scotland.

A MEDIEVAL PAINTING OF THE BURIAL OF VICTIMS OF THE BLACK DEATH

In 1326, the Count of Flanders, carrying out the orders of King Philip VI of France, arrested and imprisoned all Englishmen in Flanders. Edward III, the king of England, promptly struck back. He stopped the trade in woolens with Flanders, bring the Flemish woolen industry close to ruin. He then claimed the throne of France, insisting that he had more of a right to it than Philip. The Flemish townsmen, who had always hated being under the thumb of France, threw their support to Edward, and in 1340 he took the title of King of France.

But the title itself meant nothing; to make good his claim, Edward would have to invade France. To keep him from landing troops on the coast of Flanders, the French gathered a fleet of ships at Sluys, the harbor for the city of Bruges in Belgium. On June 25, 1340, English ships completely destroyed the French fleet and won mastery of the sea that would last for thirty years.

THE ENGLISH OVERWHELMED THE FRENCH FLEET IN THE BATTLE OF SLUYS,
OPENING THE WAY FOR THE INVASION OF NORMANDY FIVE YEARS LATER.

THE ENGLISH LONGBOWS ENDED THE ERA OF THE KNIGHT ON HORSEBACK.

For five years there was a little land fighting that decided nothing, but in 1346 the English landed at Normandy and began marching inland. The French rushed to stop them, and the two enemies met at the city of Crécy. The French army, which greatly outnumbered the English, included many powerful nobles. Among them was King John of Bohemia and his son Charles.

Against the French, the English used the new weapon, the longbow, and the new battle formation they had already tested against the Scots—two long wings of archers protected by men-at-arms on foot. As the mounted French knights charged, a storm of English arrows came whistling at them, and men and horses fell to the ground. In their heavy suits of armor, weighing as much as two hundred pounds, the knights were all but helpless, and they were killed by the hundreds. Again and again the French knights charged—and again and again they were brought down by the English archers.

King John of Bohemia, old and blind, refused to retreat. He ordered his knights to lead him into battle so that "he should have one fair blow at the English." It was no use: his courage only brought him death. By the time night fell, the French, the strongest military power in Europe, had been thoroughly defeated. England had taught the world that the knight on horseback no longer ruled the battlefield, although a century would pass before the French took the lesson to heart.

The English followed up their victory at Crécy by laying siege to Calais, an important seaport in northern France. When the city finally fell, in 1347, the English drove out the French towns-men and brought in English colonists. Besides opening the way into France, England now had a new market to take the place of Flanders.

The war was interrupted by the terrible plague known as the Black Death, and it was not until 1356 that fighting broke out again. Led by Edward III's son, who was called the Black Prince

EDWARD'S SON WAS CALLED THE BLACK PRINCE BECAUSE OF HIS BLACK ARMOR.

JOAN OF ARC

dollars. Although John was well-meaning, he was not a good king, and many people said he wasn't worth that much money.

Nevertheless, John agreed to the ransom and in 1360, at the village of Brétigny, he signed a treaty with Edward. Edward gave up his claim to the French throne. In return, besides the ransom, England was given a large slice of France, including the provinces of Poitou, Guienne, and Gascony. John died four years later, but not before he had done something which would cause trouble to France for years to come. He made his son Philip duke of the Free County of Burgundy. As heads of an independent state, the rulers of Burgundy would prove to be dangerous rivals to the monarchy of France.

Edward, too, made a mistake when he appointed his son, the Black Prince, as governor of England's newly won territories in France. The Black Prince was no match for Charles V, who became king of France after the death of John. With the help of his constable, Bertrand du Guesclin, Charles won back much of the land that had been given to England.

Serious fighting broke out again in 1415, when Henry V was king of England. France was now torn by civil war between the Burgundians and the supporters of the French monarchy, and Henry decided to take advantage of the situation. After making sure that the Burgundians would not oppose him, he landed on the coast of Normandy with an army of 12,000 men, 8,000 of whom were archers. He began marching north, and near the village of Agincourt the French tried to stop him.

Again the French outnumbered the English, again the French relied on mounted knights in armor, again the knights were brought down by the English arrows and slaughtered. Like Crécy and Poitiers, the battle of Agincourt ended in a complete victory for the English and a triumph of archers over mounted knights.

The English went on to conquer Normandy, and in May of 1420, they and the French signed the Treaty of Troyes, which named Henry as the heir to the French throne. To seal the bargain, Henry married Catherine, the daughter of the French king, Charles VI. In 1422, however, Henry V died. The new English king, Henry VI, was an infant, and a regent ruled in his place. A few months later, the French king died, leaving as his heir Charles VII.

because of his custom of wearing black armor, the English again overwhelmed the French, this time at Poitiers. King John II of France was captured, along with many noblemen, and was taken to England to be held for ransom. The English treated him as a guest, even giving him ample spending money. And easy-going, pleasure-loving John, who prefered gambling and hunting to the duties of ruling a country, thoroughly enjoyed his stay in England.

Meanwhile, however, English soldiers were staging raids in France, and Frenchmen found life hard in their disorganized land. To make matters worse, many French nobles tried to restrict the peasants and get more work out of them, and in 1358 the peasants rose in revolt. They were put down by troops still loyal to the crown. John realized that it was high time he returned home, and he agreed to pay—or rather that France would pay—an enormous ransom: 4,000,000 gold crowns, or about thirty million

Charles was only nineteen years old, and weak and sickly besides. He was terrified of the English, and had no control of his courtiers. They took bribes, stole government money, and insulted Charles to his face. While they made themselves rich and lived in luxury, Charles shambled about in shabby clothes and could not even afford to buy a pair of good shoes. As a ruler, Charles was a joke—and the truth was that he was not yet officially the king. Although he was the heir to the throne, he had never been crowned, because the English held the city of Rheims, and the French would acknowledge no man as their king until he was crowned and consecrated in the Rheims cathedral.

In 1424, in violation of the Treaty of Troyes, the English pushed into central France. They then turned south to invade Charles' domain, and began their campaign by laying siege to the city of Orleans, on the Loire river, about eighty miles south of Paris. Once Orleans fell, the way would be open for them to take all of southern France. And Orleans would have fallen—if it had not been for a seventeen-year-old peasant girl known as Joan of Arc.

JOAN OF ARC

Joan had lived all her life in the village of Domrémy, in the province of Vaucouleurs. Unable to read or write, she had spent her days herding cattle and sheep, and helping in the fields at harvest time. Like most of the peasants around her, Joan was religious, and often she prayed to the saints whose statues stood on pedestals in the village church. Then the saints be-

THIS MINIATURE SHOWS JOAN OF ARC AT THE SIEGE OF ORLEANS.

gan to appear to Joan in visions, and she heard their voices speaking to her. The voices told her that she had a mission to perform. She must go to King Charles and take him to Rheims to be crowned, and she must drive the English out.

"I am a poor girl," Joan said. "I do not know how to ride or fight."

"It is God who commands," said the voices.

Time after time the voices spoke to her, and at last she went to the commander of the French garrison at Vaucouleurs. At first he laughed at her, but she persuaded him to give her an escort of six soldiers so that she could get to Chinon, where Charles was holding court. Dressed in soldier's clothes, she traveled three hundred miles through territory held by the English and their Burgundain allies.

At Chinon, Charles and his court were both amused and amazed at this simple peasant girl who said that God had sent her to save France. But they were impressed by her sincerity, and Charles turned her over to a committee of churchmen. After questioning and observing her for three weeks, the committee reported that she was indeed good and honest, and might well have been chosen by God to carry out his will.

Meanwhile, the English were still besieging Orleans, and the king's counselors were desperate. If Joan could do nothing else, perhaps she could put some spirit into the French troops; at any rate, there was no harm in trying. Charles gave Joan a horse, a suit of white armor, and a banner on which she inscribed her motto: "Jesus and Mary." Leading a small body of troops, she joined the army at Orleans.

The rough French soldiers soon began to look upon her as a saint. She was with them when, in 1429, they attacked the English outside Orleans. As a chronicler later wrote, "Before she came, two hundred Englishmen used to drive five hundred Frenchmen before them. After her coming, two hundred Frenchmen could beat and chase five hundred Englishmen." Although Joan knew nothing about warfare, she took part in the battle, and was wounded in the shoulder by an arrow. Inspired by her courage and daring, the French fought fiercely; they freed the city and forced the English to retreat.

Joan remained with the army while it cleared the English and Burgundians out of the Loire valley. The French commanders wanted to move north against Paris, but Joan insisted that Charles

must first be brought to the cathedral at Rheims for his coronation. And in July of 1429, while Joan stood proudly beside him, holding her banner, Charles was crowned and consecrated. Kneeling before him, Joan said, "Gentle King, now is fulfilled the will of God that I should raise the siege of Orleans, and lead you to the city of Rheims to receive the holy coronation, to show that you are indeed the king, and the rightful lord of the realm of France."

But Joan was still not satisfied; every Englishman must be driven off French soil. And Charles, who did not care for war and only wanted to live quietly and in peace, was prepared to negotiate

with the English and the Burgundians. More and more, he found Joan a nuisance. Anxious to be rid of her, he left her to fight on with anyone willing to follow her banner. In May of 1430, during the siege of Compiègne, she was captured by the Burgundians, who sold her to the English for 10,000 pounds.

The English were delighted. They were eager to show that Joan was a witch; after all, what else could explain how she had so suddenly turned the tide of the war? Only by witchcraft could an ignorant peasant girl have rallied the French troops. And those Englishmen who had little belief in witchcraft were willing enough to use

it as an excuse to destroy the person who had unified the French against them. Once Joan was dead, perhaps the English soldiers would regain their confidence and go in to victory. The English turned her over to certain representatives of the Church, who placed her on trial in Rouen on charges of heresy and sorcery.

These men had been deeply disturbed by Joan. According to them, she challenged the authority of the Church when she claimed to have received a message from God through the voices of the saints. They insisted that only priests could interpret the will of God to man. They could not allow anyone to claim personal communion with

THE ENGLISH AT ORLEANS USED CANNON AGAINST THE FORTIFIED CITY.

JOAN OF ARC WAS CONVICTED OF WITCHCRAFT AND HERESY BY A CHURCH COURT.

God. This was heresy, the kind of belief which was beginning to arise in Europe, and which the Inquisition had been organized to put down. Besides, the Bishop of Beauvais, who conducted the trial, was under control of the English, who wanted Joan dead.

"WE HAVE BURNED A SAINT!"

No help came to Joan from Charles. She had made him a king, but then she had become an embarrassment to him, and he was glad to have her off his hands. No help came to her from anyone. Alone, day after day, for ten weeks, she faced her inquisitors, who tried to get her to confess. They asked her question after question. They showed her torture instruments which they could use, they threatened her with burning at the stake. But she could still live. If only she repented and admitted her guilt, she would be sentenced to life imprisonment—and she would save her immortal soul.

At last, weary and confused, Joan signed a confession she scarcely understood. The next day she disowned it. She could not be untrue to herself and her faith. "Whatever I have said was from fear," she said. "I told you the truth of everything at the trial."

SHE WAS THEN TURNED OVER TO THE ENGLISH, WHO BURNED HER AT THE STAKE.

She was immediately sentenced to death, and on May 30, 1431, she was burned at the stake in the marketplace of Rouen. As the flames rose, she gazed upon a crucifix and called on the name of Jesus. An English soldier who watched her die cried out, "We are lost! We have burned a saint!" The English soldier was later proved to be right. In 1456 the Church re-examined her trial, condemned the court, and found her not guilty of the charges of witchcraft and heresy; in 1920 she was declared a saint.

After Joan's death, the long war dragged on. In 1435 the Duke of Burgundy broke with his English allies and signed a peace treaty with the French. The following year, a French army re-captured the great city of Paris. In 1439 the Estates General gave Charles the right to raise troops and to tax the people directly. This not only strengthened the French monarch enormously, but also allowed Charles to carry out a thorough reorganization of the army. By 1449 the French had the finest artillery in Europe, and Charles renewed the war against the English. In four years the English were almost completely driven off French soil; all that they could manage to keep in their hands was Calais.

And so, in 1453, the Hundred Years' War came to an end—but France now had a new rival, the powerful state of Burgundy. This state had come into being in 1363, when King John II of

CHARLES THE RASH OF BURGUNDY WAS THE CHIEF RIVAL OF LOUIS OF FRANCE.

was one of the richest and most splendid in Europe, and the Burgundian dukes were ambitious. They hoped to extend their territories and establish a kingdom.

When war broke out between France and Burgundy, the king of France was Louis XI. He was far different from any of the monarchs France had had before him. Homely, with long, thin legs, and a sharp-nosed face that usually wore a sour expression, Louis had no use for luxury and court ceremony. He wore shabby black clothes and a felt hat with images of the saints fastened around the crown. Louis was as practical in religion as he was in everything else; in return for his prayers, he expected the saints to give him help when he needed it.

Because he was always weaving plots and had a network of spies who reported to him, Louis was known as the Spider. He spent a great deal of time traveling about his country, poking his long nose into anything he felt concerned him. He stayed with members of the middle class rather than with his nobles; in fact, he relied on the middle class for support more than he did on the nobility. Louis believed he could gain more by negotiation and scheming than by battles, and he had good reason to think so. In spite of his strange habits, he was shrewd and crafty, and a master of diplomacy.

A UNIFIED FRANCE

Louis' enemy, Charles the Rash of Burgundy, was everything Louis was not. He was handsome, chivalrous, courteous—and stupid. Louis outwitted him, playing for time, negotiating, making treaties, buying off Burgundy's allies, until finally, in 1477, Charles was killed in the battle of Nancy. His skull was split open, and his fleeing soldiers left his body to freeze in the mud. Louis snatched up Burgundy and some of Charles' other territories. Louis' great task of expanding and unifying France was completed by his heir, Charles VIII, late in the fifteenth century. Although the French monarchs would still have to fight to hold their power, they had thrown off the customs and practices of feudalism.

France had given it as a fief to his son. By conquest, by treaty, and by marriage, the Burgundian fief grew until it included all of Flanders and the Low Countries, which would later be known as Holland and Belgium. The Burgundian court

518

THE DUKE OF YORK PLUCKS A WHITE ROSE, SYMBOL OF HIS HOUSE.

The Rise of Nationalism

1272-1485

JOAN OF ARC did more than inspire the French to drive out the English; her words and actions helped to advance a new idea. During most of the Middle Ages, people did not think of themselves as belonging to a nation. They thought of themselves as members of a church and subjects of a lord. Then, as trade increased, as towns and cities grew, as merchants' and craftsmen's guilds were formed, the forms of society began to change. The barons began to lose some of their power, while the kings gained more. Gradually, people began to think of themselves as part of a nation, and a new idea rose—the idea of nationalism.

Joan fought not for a single lord or a single community. She fought for France as a whole, for France as a nation, and her allegience was to the king as head of that nation. It was this, as much as her success on the battlefield, that frightened the barons of England and made the nobles of France uneasy. They realized that once the idea of nationalism took hold, feudalism would be done for, and they with it.

Nationalism grew stronger as kings grew stronger; a strong monarch unified his people and gave them a feeling of belonging to a nation. But the barons did not give up their power easily, and often there were rivals for the throne. In England this led to along period of conflict known as the Wars of the Roses, which lasted from 1455 to 1485. The name came from the emblems of the two families that fought to rule England. The emblem of the house of York was a white rose; the emblem of the house of Lancaster, a red rose.

The causes of the struggle between the two families went far back into the past. In the year 1272, Edward I of the Plantagenet family came to the throne. As capable as he was ambitious, Edward limited the power of his feudal barons, fought two successful wars against Scotland, and tried to unite all Britain under his rule. But Edward's greatest achievement was strengthening and systematizing the law of the land. During his reign, too, began the development of the English Parliament. At first a council of officials and advisers, in time it would become a law-making body of nobles and commoners with more power than the king.

Edward's son, Edward II, was weak and a poor ruler. In 1314, while he was on the throne, Robert Bruce led the Scots to victory over England in the battle of Bannockburn. Scotland became an independent nation and would not again be joined to England until the seventeenth century.

WARS OF THE ROSES

A third Edward took the throne in 1327. He loved jousting, hunting, and making war, and was the victor at the battles of Sluys and Crécy in the Hundred Years' War. His court was one of splendor, with much feasting and pageantry, and to his subjects he was everything that a king should be. Edward III was followed by his eleven-year-old grandson, Richard II. His uncles ruled until he was old enough to take the throne

himself; when he did, he quarreled constantly with Parliament and his nobles. In 1399, a group of his barons forced him to give up the throne, and young Henry IV, of the house of Lancaster, was made king.

Although Henry owed his crown to the nobles, he had trouble with them through most of his reign. His successor, Henry V, renewed the war with France, partly to keep his nobles busy. His victories, especially the one at Agincourt, made him popular with the people, but he died after reigning for only nine years. His infant son, Henry VI, became king, and the child's uncle, John, Duke of Bedford, was appointed regent.

Without a strong monarch to control them, the nobles were soon very powerful. To get the laws they wanted, they bribed officials and bought Paliamentary elections, and orderly government

ROBERT BRUCE'S VICTORY AT BANNOCK-
BURN GAVE SCOTLAND INDEPENDENCE.

all but broke down. To make things still worse, the French, inspired by Joan of Arc, pushed the English out of all their French territories except Calais.

Henry VI was a weak king, and the people were discontented. The house of York, led by Richard, Duke of York, plotted to push Henry off the throne, and so began the struggle for the crown which was known as the Wars of the Roses. Both the Yorkists and their enemies, the Lancastrians, raised armies, and they fought a bloody battle at St. Albans in 1455. The Yorkists won the battle, but they were unable to push out Henry.

RICHARD III AND THE TUDORS

Five years later, the Lancastrians won a battle at Wakefield, and in the fighting the Duke of York was killed. In 1461, Yorkists led by the Earl of March defeated the Lancastrians, and

KING RICHARD III

King Henry VI was forced into exile. The Earl marched to London at the head of his victorious army and took the throne as Edward IV. After several more battles, the house of York was in full control of the central government.

Edward IV was a popular king, but he died at the age of forty. The throne went to his twelve-year-old son, Edward V, and the boy's uncle, Richard of Gloucester, was named regent. Richard had the boy king and his younger brother

held as prisoners in the Tower of London, and had himself proclaimed King Richard III. The two boys were smothered to death, and most people thought that Richard had ordered the murder to make his reign more secure. For centuries Richard was known as one of the most wicked kings in English history, and Shakespeare depicted him as a hunchbacked villain who lived only to do evil. It is only in recent years that historians have begun to doubt that he killed the two young princes; they believe he owes his reputation to the stories spread by his enemies, the Tudors, long after his death.

Evil or not, Richard was unable to control the barons who opposed him, and in 1485 Henry Tudor, the Earl of Richmond, came out of exile in France to launch a revolt against him. Henry's troops met Richard's at Bosworth Field, and the battle ended with Richard dead and his gold crown on the head of Henry.

HENRY TUDOR SEIZED THE THRONE AFTER KILLING RICHARD III AT BOSWORTH.

out throughout western Europe. Kings were slowly gaining the upper hand in their struggle for power with the nobles. They encouraged the growth of towns, and more and more they looked to the middle class for their trusted advisers and officials. They established royal courts of justice to take the place of the feudal courts, and direct taxation to take the place of feudal payments and duties, which often had to be collected by force. They created national armies of paid soldiers, and no longer relied on the nobles to furnish troops.

Warfare itself was changing. New weapons and new tactics were making knights in armor, trained for hand-to-hand combat, a thing of the past, and this, too, added to the power of the kings. Even more important, manorialism, with its self-sufficient communities, its nobles and peasants and serfs, was breaking down, giving way to the freer society of towns and cities with their merchants and craftsmen.

The Black Death, the great plague that killed perhaps a third of the population of Europe, hastened the end of manorialism. The plague wiped out entire noble families; their lands then went to the kings, who redistributed them.

The rise of trade and commerce offered men new ways of obtaining money and power, and led to new classes of society. Merchants and traders helped to spread new ideas, as well as goods, throughout Europe, and they needed a strong central authority to ensure law and order. The kings were winning the loyalty of the people, who looked to them for the protection and security that had formerly come only from the feudal lords.

As feudal kingdoms became nations, each with its own identity, customs, and language, the spirit of nationalism challenged the unity of the Church. The universal Catholic Church had dominated the early Middle Ages, dictating to king and nobleman and commoner alike. But as feudalism declined, the authority of the kings became greater and greater.

With the end of feudalism came the end of the Middle Ages. A new kind of society was in the making, a society that would change Europe's ways of living and thinking and bring about new systems of government.

Henry came to the throne as Henry VII, and to strengthen his position married Edward IV's daughter. He took as his emblem the Tudor rose of red and white, which combined the white rose of York and the red rose of Lancaster. The Battle of Bosworth field marked the end of the Wars of the Roses and the beginning of England's line of Tudor kings.

It also marked the end of feudalism in England. As a matter of fact, feudalism had begun to die

523

IMPORTANT DATES AND EVENTS

1170 Thomas á Becket, archbishop of Canterbury, is murdered.

1189 Frederick Barbarossa, Richard the Lion-Hearted, and Philip of France join the third crusade.

1190 Frederick dies in Asia Minor.

1204 Constantinople is sacked by the fourth crusade.

1212 The children's crusade.

1214 John of England loses his French possessions at the battle of Bouvines.

1215 The English barons force John to sign Magna Carta; the Dominican monks are recognized.

1223 The Franciscan order of monks is recognized by the pope.

1233 The Inquisition is established in Rome.

1265 Simon de Montfort calls the first English Parliament.

1302 Philip the Fair of France calls the first meeting of the Estates General.

1338 The Hundred Years War between England and France begins.

1340 England destroys the French fleet at the battle of Sluys.

1346 England invades Normandy; The English win the battle of Crecy

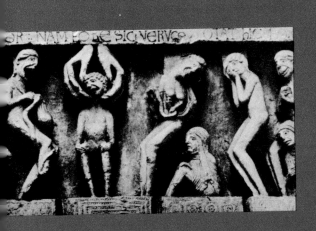

IN THE MIDDLE AGES, 1170-1485

by the use of the long bow.

1347 The English capture and settle Calais.

1356 The English overwhelm the French at Poitiers and capture King John of France.

1415 The English under King Henry V defeat the French at Agincourt and conquer Normandy.

1420 The Treaty of Troyes gives England much of France and recognizes Henry as the next French king.

1422 Death of Henry V.

1429 French troops under Joan of Arc lift the English siege of Orleans; Charles VII is crowned king of France at Rheims.

1431 The English burn Joan of Arc at the stake as a heretic.

1453 End of the Hundred Years War.

1455-1485 The Wars of the Roses between the houses of York and Lancaster.

1477 Louis XI defeats Charles of Burgundy and begins to unify the kingdom of France.

1485 Henry Tudor defeats King Richard III at Bosworth Field to win the crown of England.